Miles

The Companion Guide to the Miles Davis Autobiography

Miles

The Companion Guide to the Miles Davis Autobiography

Marc Antomattei

Marc Antomattei Press
Tokyo, Japan

MARC ANTOMATTEI PRESS

Published by Marc Antomattei Press™
marcantomatteiproductions@gmail.com

Designed & written by Marc Antomattei
Cover photograph by Gilles Larrain
Pen and ink drawing by Caesar Antomattei
Photos by Marc Antomattei
DJ photograph by Mewan Pradeep
Assisting Editor David Gregory

ISBN-13: 978-0-9846391-6-8 (Hardcover)
ISBN-13: 978-0-9846391-7-5 (Paperback)
ISBN-13: 978-0-9846391-8-2 (eBook)
ISBN-13: 978-0-9846391-1-3 (Audio Book)

TABLE OF CONTENTS

INTRODUCTION

THE MILES DAVIS COMPANION GUIDE

APPENDIX

TABLE OF CONTENTS

INTRODUCTION ON THE REVISION

Welcome to the revised edition of the Miles Davis autobiography companion guide. It's almost the tenth anniversary of the release of this book. The big question we'll get right into without delay. Why am I revising this book, and what's the difference between it and the original version? If you're an author and only make small changes to your publication, like fixing typographical errors, etc., it doesn't call for or is considered a revision. Though, in my case, I'm making very noticeable changes, the kind that requires associating a new ISBN with it. The most significant change made is the font size.

The original book was only 68 pages in length, and it was thin like a pancake. That was due to me using an unorthodox 9 point font size throughout the book. The smallest font size typically used in books is 10 pt, with 14 pt being the maximum, and 12 pt being the average. I intentionally set it up that way because it made the book's typography aesthetically pleasing when glancing at pages in their entire scope. I did the book's layout and typesetting from a graphic designer's viewpoint. I was too concerned with seeing how I could literally make the flow and organization of text beautiful. But once you start reading it, even if not for myself personally, I can understand how it can be straining on some older readers' eyes. This revision's general font size is now 11, although you can still find some smaller fonts in the annotated tunes & album listing section and the buyer's guide & appraisal section.

Aside from changes to the font size that increased the page count some twenty-plus pages, I also did the small things such as correct minor grammatical mistakes. I then tried to change as many passive voice sentences into the active voice for a more direct, educated reading experience, using passive voice only in moderation. The final thing is, I wrote and included a very controversial article in the previous edition as an opinion piece. I still share the same viewpoints today on that matter, and while the easy thing to do would have been to remove it for readers that get uncomfortable easily, I decided to include it again along with a retort to my critics. If this is your first time here, I hope you find this collector's experience to your satisfaction.

INTRODUCTION ON HOW THIS BOOK CAME TO BE

The idea struck me to make this book when I read Miles Davis' autobiography for the first time. Initially, I thought, "How cool would it be if there were a soundtrack to accompany the book?" Knowing though that the world has cats and dogs in it that won't get along nicely (speaking of the various labels Miles has worked for), the chances of there being an official release of something like that is exceptionally slim. So that idea was out the window. Then after reading a bit more is when I came upon another ingenious idea.

Miles' massive four hundred plus page autobiography is part discography, in my opinion, because he references so many tunes and albums he and others made. He also goes into further detail by providing recording dates and mentioning who accompanied him on those dates. I was about one-third done with reading the book when I read what Miles had to say about an alto saxophone player by the name of Jackie McLean. Miles said, "Jackie could play his ass off," but he also said Jackie always fucked up when playing a tune called "Yesterdays." Miles said, "He never played it right" and had to tell Jackie to sit out on playing during the recording session.

I, for one, had never heard the tune "Yesterdays" before, and I wanted to know what it sounded like so that I could try to understand further how difficult it must have been for Jackie to play and why Miles was so upset. I actually would like to hear every single tune Miles references in his autobiography. So from reading that part, in particular, is when the idea struck me to make an annotated guide citing all the tunes in the autobiography in the order that Miles mentions them. This is so that the reader, myself included, can easily find the album in our collections that the tune spoken of appears on. And if we (us Miles Davis fanatics) don't have the song, should we decide to, we could buy the single .mp3 or .wav file from a source like Amazon or iTunes fairly easily, or for completest (like myself) we can buy the entire album it appears on. I thought it would merely be a great idea to simultaneously listen to the tune spoken of in the book as I am reading it.

This is the official soundtrack to Miles Davis' life. For those real Miles Davis aficionados, the ideal thing to do would be to go through this guide, which I have made and compile a custom soundtrack to the autobiography. I can tell you it's possible, but it will be expensive.

MILES & ME – WHY I'M A FAN

When I was a teenager and my brother Miguel was a young adult, we got turned on to jazz music (and it was the start of a beautiful relationship between us and the music). When we frequented the 1,200,000 square foot shopping mall Opry Mills in Nashville, Tennessee, we always stopped by (at the time) Tower Records. They had a fine jazz section in their massive store, and we would spend hours upon hours delving into the music and usually took something home with us that night.

For jazz music, I have always been a sucker for the trumpet and its flare. Before I ever knew or really could conceive just how big Miles Davis was in the jazz world (by listeners, by critics, by sales), he was at the top of my list for favorites. Today he remains my favorite jazz musician of all-time, and I place him within my top four geniuses of music with Michael Jackson, Stevie Wonder, and John Williams.

Now I am 28 (as of Jan. 2011), and I have dedicated my life to music. I am a professional DJ residing in Tokyo, Japan, a connoisseur of music. Given the right type of party that hires me, I am sure to be found playing Miles Davis tunes spanning many different eras for 1) because it sounds great! 2) Because I always am trying to spread the gospel and educate people about his music.

I am, in fact, an official Miles Davis connoisseur. Miles Davis is the birth of cool, and I credit a lot of my image to have come from what he has done before me. I also have self-proclaimed myself as "the Miles Davis of DJs," and I am immensely proud of that.

HOW TO READ AND USE THIS BOOK

This book is based entirely on the unabridged Simon & Schuster American hardcover and paperback editions of "Miles: The Autobiography." The content in both of those editions is the same, including the layout and page numbering. I don't believe this to be the case. Still, possibly the page numbers themselves might not be parallel with each other between the American Simon & Schuster versions and that of the UK paperback edition from 1990 (Picador Books). However, the UK Picador edition might be licensed from Simon & Schuster. It could appear the same textually with possibly only the title page or copyright page varying from its US counterpart. The Japanese edition, that's split into two volumes, is irrelevant due to language and writing character differences. The final thing to note is that citing the page numbers from the autobiography is an integral part of my book. All my information is collected and displayed sequentially in the order that Miles mentions it, corresponding to the page numbers in the autobiography.

I will cite a tune mentioned within the pages of the autobiography as such:

*Page #   Artist Name – Tune Title

   (Album Title in parenthesis)(**RVG)[Record Label in brackets]

I will cite an album title mentioned with no reference to any particular tune as follows:

*Page #   (Album Title/Album Artist Name in parenthesis)[Record Label in brackets]

---

*Page number the tune or album mentioned can be found in "Miles – The Autobiography," written by Miles Davis with Quincy Troupe.

**(RVG) Rudy Van Gelder Remastered CD

N/A means a search for an album or tune title with that title mentioned came up empty.

If known that an album existed before but may no longer be in print and if a newer album containing the same content has been released, but with a different title, both the new album title and the original album title are cited.

MILES: THE AUTOBIOGRAPHY ANNOTATED TUNES & ALBUM LISTING

PROLOGUE

7   Dizzy Gillespie – Woody'n You

(Album: Showtime at the Spotlite, 52nd Street, New York City 1946) [Label: Uptown Jazz]

7   Jay McShann – Hootie Blues

(Album: Last of Blue Devils)[Label: Koch Jazz]

9   Sarah Vaughan – You Are My First Love

(Album: N/A)[Label: N/A]

CHAPTER 2

36   Billy Eckstine – Airmail Special

(Album: Airmail Special)[Label: Drive Archive]

37   Ike Quebec – Intermezzo

(Album: The Complete Blue Note 45 Sessions)[Label: Blue Note]

37   Fats Waller – Honeysuckle Rose

(Album: The Very Best of Fats Waller)[Label: Collector's Choice]

37   Charlie Parker – Honeysuckle Rose

(Album: A Studio Chronicle 1940-1948)[Label: JSP]

37   John Coltrane – Body and Soul

(Album: Coltrane's Sound)[Label: Atlantic]

37   Charlie Parker – Body and Soul

(Album: A Studio Chronicle 1940-1948)[Label: JSP]

CHAPTER 3

61   Miles Davis – Confirmation

(Album: Complete Birdland Recordings)[Label: Definitive Spain]

62   Miles Davis – Confirmation

(Album: Complete Birdland Recordings)[Label: Definitive Spain]

63   Art Tatum – Tea for Two

(Album: Tea for Two)[Label: Phantom]

72   Charlie Parker – Cherokee

(Album: A Studio Chronicle 1940-1948)[Label: JSP]

(Original Album: Charlie Parker's Reboppers)[Label: Savoy]

72   Charlie Parker/Miles Davis – A Night in Tunisia

13

(Original Album: Charlie Parker All Stars)[Label: Savoy]

105   (Album: Complete Savoy & Dial Recordings/Miles Davis)[Label: Definitive]

N/A (Original Album: Miles Davis All Stars/Miles Davis)[Label: Savoy]

105   Miles Davis – Milestones

(Album: Complete Savoy & Dial Recordings)[Label: Definitive]

(Album: Milestones)(Remastered)[Label: Columbia]

(Original Album: Miles Davis All Stars)[Label: Savoy]

105   Miles Davis – Little Willie Leaps

(Album: Complete Savoy & Dial Recordings)[Label: Definitive]

(Original Album: Miles Davis All Stars)[Label: Savoy]

105   Miles Davis – Half Nelson

(Album: Complete Savoy & Dial Recordings)[Label: Definitive]

(Original Album: Miles Davis All Stars)[Label: Savoy]

105   Miles Davis – Sippin' at Bell's

(Album: Complete Savoy & Dial Recordings)[Label: Definitive]

(Original Album: Miles Davis All Stars)[Label: Savoy]

106   N/A (Album: Charlie Parker Quintet/Charlie Parker)(With Miles Davis)

113   Charlie Parker – Cherokee

(Album: A Studio Chronicle 1940-1948)[Label: JSP]

(Original Album: Charlie Parker's Reboppers)[Label: Savoy]

117   Miles Davis – Moon Dreams

(Album: Birth of the Cool)(RVG)[Label: Blue Note]

117   Miles Davis – Boplicity

(Album: Birth of the Cool)(RVG)[Label: Blue Note]

117   (Album: Birth of the Cool/Miles Davis)(RVG)[Label: Blue Note]

118   Miles Davis – Jeru

(Album: Birth of the Cool)(RVG)[Label: Blue Note]

118   Miles Davis – Move

(Album: Birth of the Cool)(RVG)[Label: Blue Note]

118   Miles Davis – Godchild

(Album: Birth of the Cool)(RVG)[Label: Blue Note]

118   Miles Davis – Budo

(Album: Birth of the Cool)(RVG)[Label: Blue Note]

119   Miles Davis – Boplicity

(Album: Birth of the Cool)(RVG)[Label: Blue Note]

119   (Album: Birth of the Cool/Miles Davis)(RVG)[Label: Blue Note]

(Album: Workin')(24 Karat Gold Disc)[Label: DCC]

(Album: Workin' With the Miles Davis Quintet)(RVG) [Label: Prestige]

175   Miles Davis – Lazy Susan

(Album: Miles Davis, Vol. 1)[Label: Blue Note]

176   Miles Davis – Blue Haze

(Album: Blue Haze)[Label: Prestige]

177   (Album: Walkin'/Miles Davis)(RVG)[Label: Prestige]

177   (Album: Birth of the Cool/Miles Davis)(RVG)[Label: Blue Note]

178   Miles Davis – Budo

(Album: Birth of The Cool)(RVG)[Label: Blue Note]

178   Miles Davis – Move

(Album: Birth of The Cool)(RVG)[Label: Blue Note]

178   Miles Davis – Boplicity

(Album: Birth of The Cool)(RVG)[Label: Blue Note]

178   (Album: Birth of the Cool/Miles Davis)(RVG)[Label: Blue Note]

178   Ahmad Jamal – The Surrey with the Fringe on Top

(Album: Complete Recordings)[Label: Definitive Spain]

178   Ahmad Jamal – Squeeze Me

(Album: Complete Recordings)[Label: Definitive Spain]

178   Ahmad Jamal – My Funny Valentine

(Album: Cross Country Tour: 1958-1961)[Label: Verve]

178   Miles Davis – My Funny Valentine

(Album: My Funny Valentine: Miles Davis in Concert) [Label: Columbia]

(Album: Workin')(24 Karat Gold Disc)[Label: DCC]

(Album: Workin' With the Miles Davis Quintet)(RVG) [Label: Prestige]

178   Ahmad Jamal – I Don't Wanna Be Kissed

(Album: Complete Recordings)[Label: Definitive Spain]

178   Ahmad Jamal – Billy Boy

(Album: Complete Recordings)[Label: Definitive Spain]

178   Ahmad Jamal – A Gal in Calico

(Album: Complete Recordings)[Label: Definitive Spain]

178   Ahmad Jamal – Will You Still Be Mine

(Album: Complete Recordings)[Label: Definitive Spain]

178   Ahmad Jamal – But Not For Me

(Album: Complete Live at the Pershing Lounge 1958)
[Label: Gambit Spain]

178   Ahmad Jamal – Ahmad's Blues

(Album: Complete Recordings)[Label: Definitive Spain]

178   Ahmad Jamal – New Rhumba

(Album: Complete Recordings)[Label: Definitive Spain]

178   Miles Davis – New Rhumba

(Album: Miles Ahead)(Remastered)[Label: Columbia]

178   Miles Davis – But Not For Me

(Album: Bag's Groove)(RVG)[Label: Prestige]

178   Miles Davis – Airegin

(Album: Cookin')(24 Karat Gold Disc)[Label: DCC]

(Album: Cookin')(RVG)[Label: Prestige]

(Album: Bag's Groove)(RVG)[Label: Prestige]

179   Miles Davis – Doxy

(Album: Bag's Groove)(RVG)[Label: Prestige]

179   Miles Davis – Oleo

(Album: Relaxin')(24 Karat Gold Disc)[Label: DCC]

(Album: Relaxin')(RVG)[Label: Prestige]

(Album: Bag's Groove)(RVG)[Label: Prestige]

186   (Album: Miles Davis and the Modern Jazz Giants/Miles Davis)(Prestige 50th Anniversary Special Commemorative Edition)(Remastered)[Label: Prestige]

187   Miles Davis – Bemsha Swing

(Album: Miles Davis and the Modern Jazz Giants)(Prestige 50th Anniversary Special Commemorative Edition)(Remastered)
[Label: Prestige]

187   Miles Davis – The Man I Love

(Album: Miles Davis and the Modern Jazz Giants)(Prestige 50th Anniversary Special Commemorative Edition)(Remastered)
[Label: Prestige]

188   Miles Davis – Walkin'

(Album: Walkin')(RVG)[Label: Prestige]

188   Miles Davis – Blue 'N' Boogie

(Album: Walkin')(RVG)[Label: Prestige]

188   (Album: Miles Davis and the Modern Jazz Giants/Miles Davis)(Prestige 50th Anniversary Special Commemorative Edition)(Remastered)[Label: Prestige]

188   (Album: Birth of the Cool/Miles Davis)(RVG)[Label: Blue Note]

190   (Album: The Musings of Miles/Miles Davis)
(in autobiography mentioned as: Miles Davis All Stars)[Label: Prestige]

19

(Album: Miles)(Also called: The New Miles Davis Quintet)
[Label: Prestige]

201   Miles Davis – Stablemates

(Album: Miles)(24 Karat Gold Disc)[Label: DCC]

(Album: Miles)(Also called: The New Miles Davis Quintet)
[Label: Prestige]

201   Miles Davis – The Theme

(Album: Miles)(24 Karat Gold Disc)[Label: DCC]

(Album: Miles)(Also called: The New Miles Davis Quintet)
[Label: Prestige]

201   Miles Davis – S'posin

(Album: Miles)(24 Karat Gold Disc)[Label: DCC]

(Album: Miles)(Also called: The New Miles Davis Quintet)
[Label: Prestige]

203   (Album: 'Round About Midnight/Miles Davis)(Legacy Edition)
(Remastered)[Label: Columbia]

204   Miles Davis – 'Round Midnight

(Album: 'Round About Midnight)(Legacy Edition)(Remastered)
[Label: Columbia]

204   Miles Davis – Sweet Sue, Just You

(Album: Basic Miles)(1973 LP Record)[Label: Columbia]

(Album: 'Round About Midnight)(Legacy Edition)(Remastered)
[Label: Columbia]

204   (Album: Bernstein Century: Bernstein on Jazz – What is Jazz?/
Leonard Bernstein)[Label: Sony Classical]

204   Miles Davis – All of You

(Album: 'Round About Midnight)(Legacy Edition)(Remastered)
[Label: Columbia]

204   (Album: Basic Miles/Miles Davis)(1973 LP Record)[Label: Columbia]

205   (Album: Music For Brass: The 1957 Columbia Third Stream Recordings, vol.
1/The Brass Ensemble of the Jazz and Classical Music Society)
[Label: Soundmark]

205   The Brass Ensemble of the Jazz and Classical Music Society – Three Little
Feelings

(Album: A Trumpet vs. Darkness: The Leader & The Side Man)
[Label: DiscMedi S.A.]

205   Miles Davis – My Funny Valentine

(Album: Cookin')(24 Karat Gold Disc)[Label: DCC]

(Album: Cookin')(RVG)[Label: Prestige]

205   Miles Davis – If I Were a Bell

CHAPTER 11

219   (Album: Miles Davis and the Modern Jazz Giants/Miles Davis)(Prestige 50th Anniversary Special Commemorative Edition)(Remastered)[Label: Prestige]

219   Miles Davis – Bags' Groove

         (Album: Bags' Groove)(RVG)[Label: Prestige]

219   Miles Davis – The Man I Love

         (Album: Miles Davis and the Modern Jazz Giants)(Prestige 50th Anniversary Special Commemorative Edition)(Remastered) [Label: Prestige]

219   Miles Davis – Swing Spring

         (Album: Miles Davis and the Modern Jazz Giants)(Prestige 50th Anniversary Special Commemorative Edition)(Remastered) [Label: Prestige]

224   (Album: Somethin' Else/Julian "Cannonball" Adderley)(RVG) [Label: Blue Note]

224   Miles Davis – Billy Boy

         (Album: Milestones)(Remastered)[Label: Columbia]

224   Miles Davis – Straight, No Chaser

         (Album: Milestones)(Remastered)[Label: Columbia]

224   Miles Davis – Milestones

         (Album: Milestones)(Remastered)[Label: Columbia]

224   Miles Davis – Two Bass Hit

         (Album: Milestones)(Remastered)[Label: Columbia]

224   Miles Davis – Sid's Ahead

         (Album: Milestones)(Remastered)[Label: Columbia]

224   Miles Davis – Dr. Jackle (also called "Dr. Jekyll")

         (Album: Milestones)(Remastered)[Label: Columbia]

224   (Album: Milestones/Miles Davis)(Remastered)[Label: Columbia]

225   Miles Davis – Milestones

         (Album: Milestones)(Remastered)[Label: Columbia]

229   (Album: Porgy and Bess/Miles Davis)(Bonus Tracks)[Label: Columbia]

229   Miles Davis – Fran-Dance

         (Album: Jazz Track)[Label: Jazz Beat]

         (Album: The Complete Columbia Recordings)(2000) [Label: Columbia]

         (Album: The Complete Columbia Recordings 1955-1961) (2004 Reissue)[Label: Columbia]

229   Miles Davis – On Green Dolphin Street

         (Album: Jazz Track)[Label: Jazz Beat]

(Album: The Complete Columbia Recordings)(2000)
[Label: Columbia]

(Album: The Complete Columbia Recordings 1955-1961)
(2004 Reissue)[Label: Columbia]

229   Miles Davis – Stella by Starlight

(Album: Jazz Track)[Label: Jazz Beat]

(Album: The Complete Columbia Recordings)(2000)
[Label: Columbia]

(Album: The Complete Columbia Recordings 1955-1961)
(2004 Reissue)[Label: Columbia]

229   Miles Davis – Love For Sale

(Album: Jazz Track)[Label: Jazz Beat]

(Album: The Complete Columbia Recordings)(2000)
[Label: Columbia]

(Album: The Complete Columbia Recordings 1955-1961)
(2004 Reissue)[Label: Columbia]

230   (Album: Jazz Track/Miles Davis)[Label: Jazz Beat]

(Original Album: On Green Dolphin Street/Miles Davis)[Label: Columbia]

230   (Album: Elevator to the Gallows/Miles Davis)[Label: Fontana]

230   (Concert: At Newport 1958/Miles Davis)[Label: Columbia]

230   (Album: Porgy and Bess/Miles Davis)(Bonus Tracks)[Label: Columbia]

230   (Album: Birth of the Cool/Miles Davis)(RVG)[Label: Capitol/Blue Note]

230   Miles Davis – I Loves You, Porgy

(Album: Porgy and Bess)(Bonus Tracks)[Label: Columbia]

231   (Album: Porgy and Bess/Miles Davis)(Bonus Tracks)[Label: Columbia]

233   (Album: Kind of Blue/Miles Davis)(Remastered)[Label: Columbia]

(Album: Kind of Blue Deluxe 50th Anniversary Collector's Edition)
[Label: Columbia]

(Album: Kind of Blue Legacy Edition)[Label: Columbia]

233   Miles Davis – Freddie Freeloader

(Album: Kind of Blue Deluxe 50th Anniversary Collector's
Edition)[Label: Columbia]

(Album: Kind of Blue Legacy Edition)[Label: Columbia]

234   (Album: Kind of Blue/Miles Davis)(Remastered)[Label: Columbia]

(Album: Kind of Blue Deluxe 50th Anniversary Collector's Edition)
[Label: Columbia]

(Album: Kind of Blue Legacy Edition)[Label: Columbia]

234   (Album: Milestones/Miles Davis)(Remastered)[Label: Columbia]

234   Maurice Ravel – Concerto for the Left Hand and Orchestra

23

(Album: Piano Concerto for the Left Hand in D major, Piano Concerto in G major; Faure: Ballade, Op. 19)[Label: Chandos]

234   Sergei Rachmaninoff – Concerto No. 4

(Rachmaninoff: Complete Works For Piano and Orchestra) [Label: Philips]

235   (Album: Kind of Blue/Miles Davis)(Remastered)[Label: Columbia]

(Album: Kind of Blue Deluxe 50th Anniversary Collector's Edition) [Label: Columbia]

(Album: Kind of Blue Legacy Edition)[Label: Columbia]

235   Miles Davis – All Blues

(Album: Kind of Blue Deluxe 50th Anniversary Collector's Edition)[Label: Columbia]

(Album: Kind of Blue Legacy Edition)[Label: Columbia]

235   Miles Davis – So What

(Album: Kind of Blue Deluxe 50th Anniversary Collector's Edition)[Label: Columbia]

(Album: Kind of Blue Legacy Edition)[Label: Columbia]

236   Billie Holiday – I Loves You Porgy

(Album: Greatest Hits)[Label: GRP]

236   (Album: Giant Steps/John Coltrane)(Deluxe Edition)(Remastered) [Label: Atlantic]

236   (Album: Kind of Blue/Miles Davis)(Remastered)[Label: Columbia]

(Album: Kind of Blue Deluxe 50th Anniversary Collector's Edition) [Label: Columbia]

(Album: Kind of Blue Legacy Edition)[Label: Columbia]

241   (Album: Sketches of Spain/Miles Davis)[Label: Columbia]

(Album: Sketches of Spain 50th Anniversary 2CD Legacy Edition) [Label: Columbia]

241   Joaquin Rodrigo – Concierto de Aranjuez

(Album: Rodrigo: Complete Concertos for Guitar and Harp) [Label: Philips]

241   Miles Davis – Concierto de Aranjuez

(Album: Sketches of Spain)(Remastered)[Label: Columbia]

(Album: Sketches of Spain 50th Anniversary 2CD Legacy Edition) [Label: Columbia]

241   Miles Davis – The Pan Piper

(Album: Sketches of Spain)(Remastered)[Label: Columbia]

(Album: Sketches of Spain 50th Anniversary 2CD Legacy Edition) [Label: Columbia]

241   Miles Davis – Saeta

25

(Album: Sketches of Spain 50th Anniversary 2CD Legacy Edition) [Label: Columbia]

252   (Album Cover: Someday My Prince Will Come)(Features: Frances Taylor) [Label: Columbia]

252   (Album Cover: Filles de Kilimanjaro)(Features: Betty Mabry)[Label: Columbia]

252   (Album Cover: Sorcerer)(Features: Cicely Tyson)[Label: Columbia]

252   (Album Cover: Miles Davis at the Fillmore)(Features: Marguerite Eskridge) [Label: Columbia]

252   Miles Davis – Pfrancing

         (Album: Someday My Prince Will Come)(Remastered) [Label: Columbia]

253   (Album: Miles Davis in Person Friday and Saturday Nights at the Blackhawk, Complete/Miles Davis)[Label: Columbia]

253   (Album: Miles Davis at Carnegie Hall/Miles Davis)[Label: Columbia]

253   (Album: Sketches of Spain/Miles Davis)(Remastered)[Label: Columbia]

         (Album: Sketches of Spain 50th Anniversary 2CD Legacy Edition) [Label: Columbia]

259   (Album: Quiet Nights/Miles Davis/Gil Evans)[Label: Columbia]

260   (Album: Quiet Nights/Miles Davis/Gil Evans)[Label: Columbia]

262   (Album: Kind of Blue/Miles Davis)(Remastered)[Label: Columbia]

         (Album: Kind of Blue Deluxe 50th Anniversary Collector's Edition) [Label: Columbia]

         (Album: Kind of Blue Legacy Edition)[Label: Columbia]

263   Miles Davis – Seven Steps to Heaven

         (Album: Seven Steps to Heaven)(Remastered)[Label: Columbia]

263   Miles Davis – Joshua

         (Album: Seven Steps to Heaven)(Remastered)[Label: Columbia]

263   (Album: Miles Davis Quintet: In St. Louis/Miles Davis)[Label: VGM]

264   Miles Davis – Milestones

         (Album: Milestones)(Remastered)[Label: Columbia]

264   (Album: Milestones/Miles Davis)(Remastered)[Label: Columbia]

264   (Album: Miles Davis in Europe/Miles Davis)(Remastered)[Label: Columbia]

264   (Album: Live at the 1963 Monterey Jazz Festival/Miles Davis Quintet) [Label: Monterey Jazz Festival]

265   (Play: The Time of the Barracuda)

         (Album: The Complete Columbia Studio Recordings/Miles Davis, Gil Evans) [Label: Columbia]

265   (Album: Quiet Nights/Miles Davis, Gil Evans)[Label: Columbia]

(Album: Nefertiti)(Remastered)[Label: Columbia]

281   (Album: Seven Steps to Heaven/Miles Davis)(Remastered)[Label: Columbia]

281   (Album Cover: E.S.P.)(Features: Frances)[Label: Columbia]

283   (Album: Miles Smiles/Miles Davis Quintet)(Remastered)[Label: Columbia]

284   (Album: Sorcerer/Miles Davis)[Label: Columbia]

285   (Album: Sorcerer/Miles Davis)[Label: Columbia]

285   (Album: Nefertiti/Miles Davis)(Remastered)[Label: Columbia]

285   (Album: Water Babies/Miles Davis)(Deluxe Edition)[Label: Columbia]

286   (Album: A Love Supreme/John Coltrane)[Label: Impulse!]

287   (Album: A Love Supreme/John Coltrane)[Label: Impulse!]

287   Duke Ellington – In The Beginning God

(Album: Concert of Sacred Music)[Label: RCA]

PHOTO PAGES 2

(Album: Milestones/Miles Davis)(Remastered)[Label: Columbia]

(Album: Kind of Blue/Miles Davis)(Remastered)[Label: Columbia]

(Album: Kind of Blue Deluxe 50th Anniversary Collector's Edition) [Label: Columbia]

(Album: Kind of Blue Legacy Edition)[Label: Columbia]

(Album: 'Round About Midnight/Miles Davis)(Remastered)[Label: Columbia]

(Album: Sketches of Spain/Miles Davis)(Remastered)[Label: Columbia]

(Album: Sketches of Spain 50th Anniversary 2CD Legacy Edition) [Label: Columbia]

(Album: E.S.P./Miles Davis)[Label: Columbia]

(Album: Sorcerer/Miles Davis)[Label: Columbia]

(Album: Filles de Kilimanjaro/Miles Davis)(Deluxe Edition) [Label: Columbia]

(Album: Miles Smiles/Miles Davis Quintet)(Remastered)[Label: Columbia]

(Album: Bitches Brew/Miles Davis)(Remastered)[Label: Columbia]

(Album: Bitches Brew: 40th Anniversary Collector's Edition) [Label: Columbia]

(Album: The Complete Bitches Brew Sessions)[Label: Columbia]

(Album: Bitches Brew Legacy Deluxe)[Label: Columbia]

(Album: On the Corner/Miles Davis)[Label Columbia]

(Album: The Complete on the Corner Sessions)[Label: Columbia]

(Album: Tutu/Miles Davis)(SHM-CD)[Label: Warner Bros.]

(Album: The Complete In A Silent Way Sessions)[Label: Columbia]

296   (Album: Kind of Blue/Miles Davis)(Remastered)[Label: Columbia]

(Album: Kind of Blue Deluxe 50th Anniversary Collector's Edition) [Label: Columbia]

(Album: Kind of Blue Legacy Edition)[Label: Columbia]

297   (Album: In A Silent Way/Miles Davis)

(Album: The Complete In A Silent Way Sessions)[Label: Columbia]

297   (Album: Bitches Brew/Miles Davis)(Remastered)[Label: Columbia]

(Album: Bitches Brew: 40th Anniversary Collector's Edition) [Label: Columbia]

(Album: The Complete Bitches Brew Sessions)[Label: Columbia]

(Album: Bitches Brew Legacy Deluxe)[Label: Columbia]

298   (Album: Bitches Brew/Miles Davis)(Remastered)[Label: Columbia]

(Album: Bitches Brew: 40th Anniversary Collector's Edition) [Label: Columbia]

(Album: The Complete Bitches Brew Sessions)[Label: Columbia]

(Album: Bitches Brew Legacy Deluxe)[Label: Columbia]

298   Cannonball Adderley - Country Preacher (Live)

(Album: Country Preacher: Live at Operation Breadbasket) [Label: Blue Note]

299   (Album: In A Silent Way/Miles Davis)

(Album: The Complete In A Silent Way Sessions)[Label: Columbia]

299   (Album: Kind of Blue/Miles Davis)(Remastered)[Label: Columbia]

(Album: Kind of Blue Deluxe 50th Anniversary Collector's Edition) [Label: Columbia]

(Album: Kind of Blue Legacy Edition)[Label: Columbia]

300   (Album: Bitches Brew/Miles Davis)(Remastered)[Label: Columbia]

(Album: Bitches Brew: 40th Anniversary Collector's Edition) [Label: Columbia]

(Album: The Complete Bitches Brew Sessions)[Label: Columbia]

(Album: Bitches Brew Legacy Deluxe)[Label: Columbia]

301   (Album: Sketches of Spain/Miles Davis)(Remastered)[Label: Columbia]

(Album: Sketches of Spain 50th Anniversary 2CD Legacy Edition) [Label: Columbia]

301   (Album: Bitches Brew/Miles Davis)(Remastered)[Label: Columbia]

(Album: Bitches Brew: 40th Anniversary Collector's Edition) [Label: Columbia]

(Album: The Complete Bitches Brew Sessions)[Label: Columbia]

(Album: Bitches Brew Legacy Deluxe)[Label: Columbia]

31

316	(Album: Live-Evil/Miles Davis)(Limited Edition Remastered) [Label: Columbia]
316	(Album: Bitches Brew/Miles Davis)(Remastered)[Label: Columbia]
	(Album: Bitches Brew: 40th Anniversary Collector's Edition) [Label: Columbia]
	(Album: The Complete Bitches Brew Sessions)[Label: Columbia]
	(Album: Bitches Brew Legacy Deluxe)[Label: Columbia]
317	(Album: Live-Evil/Miles Davis)(Limited Edition Remastered) [Label: Columbia]
317	(Album: Bitches Brew/Miles Davis)(Remastered)[Label: Columbia]
	(Album: Bitches Brew: 40th Anniversary Collector's Edition) [Label: Columbia]
	(Album: The Complete Bitches Brew Sessions)[Label: Columbia]
	(Album: Bitches Brew Legacy Deluxe)[Label: Columbia]
317	Miles Davis – What I Say
	(Album: Live-Evil)(Limited Edition Remastered)[Label: Columbia]
318	Miles Davis – Sivad
	(Album: Live-Evil)(Limited Edition Remastered)[Label: Columbia]
318	Miles Davis – Selim
	(Album: Live-Evil)(Limited Edition Remastered)[Label: Columbia]
318	(Album: Abraxas/Santana)[Label: Columbia]
318	(Album: Isle of Wight Concert/Miles Davis)(Record)[Label: DMM Cutting]
319	(Album: Live-Evil/Miles Davis)(Limited Edition Remastered) [Label: Columbia]
322	Sly & the Family Stone – Dance to the Music
	(Album: Dance to the Music)[Label: Epic]
322	Sly & the Family Stone – Stand!
	(Album: Stand!)[Label: Epic]
322	Sly & the Family Stone – Everybody Is a Star
	(Album: Greatest Hits)[Label: Epic]
322	(Album: On the Corner/Miles Davis)[Label Columbia]
	(Album: The Complete on the Corner Sessions)[Label: Columbia]
324	(Album: On the Corner/Miles Davis)[Label Columbia]
	(Album: The Complete on the Corner Sessions)[Label: Columbia]
324	(Album: Big Fun/Miles Davis)(Remastered)[Label: Columbia]
324	(Album: Bitches Brew/Miles Davis)(Remastered)[Label: Columbia]
	(Album: Bitches Brew: 40th Anniversary Collector's Edition) [Label: Columbia]

CHAPTER 17

CHAPTER 18

CHAPTER 19

This summary is the timeline of Miles Davis' life according to the pages of his autobiography. The numbers along the left margin represent the page number in the autobiography I found the information. This summary is not supposed to be a substitute for reading the actual book; it is merely an overview. If anything, if it doesn't help promote or persuade you to read the real book with all of its extreme details, then I am urging you to read it personally.

Note: The single citation below covers this section in its entirety since all the following information came from the same source. Cited in the bibliography is additional supporting information.

Davis, Miles D. 1989. *Miles: The Autobiography*. Simon & Schuster Paperbacks.

PROLOGUE

7   Miles Davis heard and performed with Dizzy Gillespie and Charlie "Yardbird/Bird" Parker for the first time in 1944 St. Louis, Missouri. They came with Billy Eckstine's band. The two men would later become Miles' idols and mentors in music.

CHAPTER 1

12   Miles Dewey Davis III was born in Alton, Illinois, on May 26, 1926.

13   Miles' father, Dr. Miles Henry Davis II, was born on March 1, 1898 (some sources, including the autobiography, say 1900) in Noble Lake, Arkansas. His mother, Cleota Henry Davis, was born in 1900 also in Arkansas.

Miles' father has three degrees. He graduated from Arkansas Baptist College in Arkansas, Lincoln University in

Pennsylvania, and the College of Dentistry at Northwestern University in Illinois.

15   Miles' brother Vernon was born on November 3, 1929, in East St. Louis, Illinois.

18   Miles enjoyed all-American sports such as baseball, basketball, boxing, and football, among others in his youth.

CHAPTER 2

30   Miles' first good noteworthy trumpet teacher was Mr. Elwood Buchanon, his music teacher at Lincoln Senior High School.

38   Miles met Irene Birth (who later became the mother of his two children Cheryl & Gregory) at his high school when he was sixteen.

39   Miles' first time having sex was with Irene.

42   Miles Davis joined his first band when he was seventeen. He was a member of "Eddie Randle's Blue Devils," also known as the "Rhumboogie Orchestra." Miles stayed in this band for one year, from 1943 to 1944.

44   The instrument called the flugelhorn was introduced to Miles by Clark Terry.

46   Miles' parents divorced in 1944. His sister Dorothy was beginning college at Fisk University in Nashville, Tennessee, and his brother Vernon was turning into a homosexual.

      Miles got Irene pregnant with their first child Cheryl.

48   Miles left Eddie Randle's band to play with a new one called "Six Brown Cats" in June 1944.

49   Finally, with no incentives to stay around and play locally, Miles left St. Louis for New York City by train in early fall 1944.

CHAPTER 3

51   In September 1944, Miles arrived in New York City.

52   When Miles first arrived in New York, he searched for Bird & Diz and could not find them.

Miles began attending school at the Juilliard School of Music.

55   Miles found Dizzy Gillespie in NYC and met with him at his apartment on Seventh Avenue in Harlem.

57   Miles found Bird in Harlem at a club called Heatwave on 145th Street.

58   Irene moved to NYC in December 1944 and moved in with Miles. Before then, Bird was living with Miles but had to move out when Irene came. Miles found Bird a place on 147th and Broadway in the same rooming house as himself.

Miles met Thelonious Monk for the first time through Bird.

60   Miles sat in and played with Bird and Diz for the first time in NYC at Minton's Playhouse.

63   Miles began drinking in 1945.

65   Miles stated about Bird, "He was the greatest alto saxophone player who ever lived" and that "he was a genius of a musician."

66   Miles' first recording date was with Herbie Fields in May 1945.

68   Dizzy Gillespie quit Charlie Parker's band due to Bird being high off heroin and missing gigs. Miles joined Bird's band in Dizzy's place.

73   In the fall of 1945, Miles quit the Juilliard School of Music.

CHAPTER 4

75   In 1945 a producer at Savoy Records asked Bird if he would make a record. Miles joined him on his recording dates.

135   Fats Navarro died on July 7, 1950, from heroin usage.

138   Miles IV was born in East St. Louis in 1950.

139   Miles, Bird, Dexter, and Art Blakey, are arrested for drugs at Burbank airport and put in jail in L.A.

140   *Down Beat* magazine wrote an article about drugs and music and mentioned Miles and Art's arrest in L.A.

      Bob Weinstock started the Prestige label in 1949.

141   Miles was acquitted arrest in January 1951.

      Metronome magazine voted Miles into its All Star Band at the end of 1950.

CHAPTER 7

143   Miles went to record his first record for Prestige in 1951.

147   Miles' second recording date with Prestige was in October 1951. In this studio session, he recorded the album the *Miles Davis All Stars*, also called *Dig*.

      The three-minute recording limit that was on 78 rpm records was coming to an end. Introduced were new 33½ rpm recordings that let artists record longer tunes at recordings sessions. Miles was one of the first people to use it.

148   For the remainder of 1951 and in early 1952, Miles began pimping prostitutes for money to support his heroin habit.

      In 1952 Miles seriously tried to get into boxing to kick his habit, but boxing trainer Bobby McQuillen refused Miles, stating he wouldn't train anyone with a drug habit.

149   After what Bobby told Miles, it brought Miles to the realization he needed help, so he called his father to come to pick him up. They went back together to East St. Louis and Millstadt, Illinois.

150   Miles began reshooting heroin while living with his father. Miles' sister Dorothy told their father what Miles was doing with the money he was lending him. When he stopped

giving money, Miles cursed out his father. Finally, his father called the police and had Miles sent to jail in Belleville, Illinois, for one week.

151 The arrest was not official without no record kept, due to Miles' father being a sheriff. After his release, Miles' father drove him to Lexington, Kentucky, to check Miles into a prison rehabilitation program. Miles had to voluntarily sign himself into the prison, which in the end, he refused to do.

152 Miles headed back to New York.

153 Miles did his first recording for Alfred Lion's Blue Note label in 1952.

156 Miles puts down the white jazz musicians saying that they are imitators of the black ones. The white critics would talk a lot about guys like Stan Getz, Dave Brubeck, Kai Winding, Lee Konitz, Lennie Tristano, and Gerry Mulligan. Miles says some of them were junkies as well, but the critics wouldn't talk about them like they did black musicians. Miles also said some of those guys were alright musicians, but certainly, they weren't innovators.

CHAPTER 8

163 Cab Calloway told many things about the musicians who were junkies to Allan Marshall, and it was published in *Down Beat* magazine (mentioned as *Ebony* magazine in the autobiography).

164 In the summer of '53, Max Roach gave Miles a couple of $100 bills outside of Birdland. Instead of using the money to buy heroin, Miles called his father and told him he's returning home again.

Miles stay was short-lived back home though, as he received a call from Max Roach saying he is driving with Charlie Mingus to Los Angeles for some gigs, and they would pass through St. Louis.

165   Miles invited them to stay a night; after, he decided to join them in California.

167   Miles met Frances Taylor on this trip (who would later become his first wife). He was introduced to her by his Californian friend name Buddy.

169   Miles retakes the bus back home to East St. Louis and Millstadt, Illinois.

170   This time, Miles was ready to kick his habit cold turkey. He stayed in his father's two-room guesthouse apartment and locked the door. He remained locked up for about seven or eight days until one day, and it was just over.

CHAPTER 9

171   Miles left for Detroit, where he stayed for about five or six months. He didn't trust himself to be back in New York just yet.

174   Miles went back to New York in February 1954.

175   Miles got in contact with Alfred Lion and Bob Weinstock to record again for Blue Note Records and Prestige, respectively.

177   Capitol Records recorded *Birth of the Cool* in 1949 and 1950 and put it out in its entirety in 1957 (some sources say 1956).

179   Miles began taking a little bit of cocaine occasionally.

180   Miles convinced boxing trainer Bobby McQuillen that he was free from drugs and could be trained and so Bobby took him in.

188   In March of 1955, Miles was put in jail on Rikers Island by Irene for not supporting their children.

        Bird died on March 12, 1955, while Miles was in jail.

192   The jazz producer George Avakian at Columbia Records wanted Miles to sign an exclusive contract, so George and

Bob Weinstock at Prestige began negotiations to release him from his former contract.

196　Miles had put together his first great quintet with John Coltrane on tenor saxophone, Philly Joe Jones on drums, Red Garland on piano, and Paul Chambers on bass.

CHAPTER 10

200　Columbia gave Miles a $4,000 advance for his first record plus $300,000 a year. Though Miles was still under contract to Prestige for another year, and he owed them four more albums. Miles had already started recording for Columbia in October 1955 while still being apart of Prestige.

The Columbia music would not release until after fulfilling the May 1956 agreement.

202　Miles had his first throat operation in early 1956, where he had a non-cancerous growth on his larynx removed. He wasn't supposed to talk for ten days, but he got into a conversation with someone and raised his voice loudly at one point, messing up his voice permanently. This incident caused his voice to have a permanent whisper to it.

Miles bought a new white Mercedes-Benz and moved to 881 Tenth Avenue nearby to 57th Street.

203　Miles and the band secretly went back to Columbia to record tracks for his first Columbia studio album *'Round About Midnight.*

At this time, Miles was making more money and could send some over to Irene to help support their kids.

204　Trumpeter Clifford Brown and pianist Richie Powell (Bud Powell's younger brother) died in a car accident on June 26, 1956.

205　Miles recorded his last four albums for Prestige in two sessions on the dates of May 11, 1956, and October 26,

1956; the albums included *Steamin'*, *Cookin'*, *Workin'*, and *Relaxin'*, released between the years 1957 to 1961.

207   John Coltrane was deep into heroin, and Miles had to let him go temporarily.

213   Paul Chambers died on January 4, 1969, of tuberculosis (Miles put it down due to too many drugs and drinking alcohol).

214   Miles fired Trane and Philly Joe Jones in March 1957, for they were too deep into drugs and causing problems for the band.

215   Miles went with Gil Evans and his orchestra into the studio in May 1957 to record the album *Miles Ahead*.

216   Trane kicked his heroin habit cold turkey by staying with his mother in Philadelphia.

217   Miles composed the music for the French film *L'Ascenseur pour l'Echafaud. Elevator to the Gallows/Frantic* US title, *Lift to the Scaffold* British title.

CHAPTER 11

224   As a favor to Julian "Cannonball" Adderley, who had just signed with Blue Note Records, Miles appears as a sideman on his first album *Somethin' Else* recorded on March 9, 1958.

225   Miles found a new piano player for his current band at the time by the name of Bill Evans after Red Garland walked out on him.

Frances Taylor had moved to New York.

227   Frances Taylor and Miles started being together more by the spring of 1958. She had moved in with Miles in his apartment on Tenth Avenue.

Miles traded in his Mercedes-Benz for a white Ferrari convertible.

Life magazine puts Miles in their international issue as someone who is doing something good for his people.

233 Coltrane was beginning to go in his own direction and started his group in 1959. Cannonball did the same. While headlining their own bands, they also played with Miles' group occasionally.

In March 1959, Miles went into the studio with his sextet, John Coltrane, Jimmy Cobb, Paul Chambers, and Cannonball Adderley to record *Kind of Blue*. Wynton Kelly appeared on one tune.

235 Billie Holiday died on July 17, 1959, from pneumonia. Her body couldn't fight the illness from being weak from so much drug abuse.

238 After finishing an Armed Forces Day broadcast, Miles walked a white lady he knew out to a cab at the Birdland club. Afterward, a white policeman approached him and told him to move on. After Miles pointed to the marquee and stated he's working there, the policeman didn't care and told Miles again to move on, or he would arrest him. While Miles stood there and looked at him a while, a detective came up from behind and hit him on the head.

240 Miles tried to sue the police department for $500,000, but his lawyer who handled the negligence suit forgot to file the claim before the statute of limitations finished.

241 Miles began working on Sketches of Spain with Gil Evans. Recording started on November 20, 1959.

CHAPTER 12

246 John Coltrane permanently quit Miles Davis' group.

251 Miles began recording *Someday My Prince Will Come* on March 7 and finished recording on March 21, 1961.

252 Miles discovered he had sickle-cell anemia, which caused him a lot of pain in his joints.

254 Miles bought a converted Russian Orthodox Church on 312 West 77th Street in 1960 and moved into it with Frances.

255 Miles was voted Best Trumpet in 1961 by *Down Beat* magazine.

256 Miles and Frances were married on December 21, 1960.

257 *Ebony* magazine did a seven-page article on Miles in January 1961.

258 Miles Davis' father dies in the spring of 1962.

259 Miles' father's funeral was in May 1962 and is one of the largest ever in East St. Louis.

260 *Playboy* magazine interviewed Miles in November 1962.

265 In 1963, Miles won another *Down Beat* magazine poll for Best Trumpet.

266 Miles Davis' mother died in Barnes Hospital in St. Louis on February 29, 1964. The funeral was at Luke's AME Church in East St. Louis.

268 Miles' daughter Cheryl was attending Columbia University, and his son Gregory was into boxing; he wanted to be a professional boxer. Shortly after this, Gregory joined the military and went to Vietnam.

269 Miles took his first trip and did his first-ever concert in Tokyo and Kyoto, Japan, in July 1964 (the autobiography mentions the second city as being Osaka instead of Kyoto).

CHAPTER 13

272 Rock 'n' roll and hard rock began replacing jazz as the most popular social music.

Wynton Kelly died on April 12, 1971, of an epileptic seizure.

278 Miles did six studio-recording dates within four years for Columbia from 1965 to 1969.

282 After many arguments, problems, and worries started by Miles, Frances finally left Miles for good.

Frances and Marlon Brando started going out.

Miles had a hip operation in April 1965; he had his hip ball replaced.

283 Miles got a liver infection in January 1966.

Miles met Cicely Tyson at Riverside Park.

284 Miles recorded *Sorcerer* from May 16 – 24, 1967.

285 Hampton Hawes dies on May 22, 1977, from a hemorrhage of the brain.

John Coltrane dies on July 17, 1967, from cirrhosis of the liver.

289 Martin Luther King, Jr. was assassinated in Memphis, Tennessee, on April 4, 1968.

290 Miles finished the album *Miles in the Sky* on May 17, 1968, and started working on *Filles de Kilimanjaro* on June 19, 1968.

Miles' had his divorce with Frances finalized in February 1968.

Miles Davis and his new girlfriend, Betty Mabry, were married in September 1968.

CHAPTER 14

292 Miles Davis' wife, Betty Mabry, turned Miles onto funkier sounding music. Miles began listening to James Brown, Jimi Hendrix, and Sly and the Family Stone.

Miles Davis met Jimi Hendrix.

293 Miles Davis' group broke up after Ron Carter left. Ron didn't want to play electric bass.

Herbie Hancock and Tony Williams wanted to leave to form their own groups.

294   Miles began using Chick Corea and Joe Zawinul for studio recordings at this time.

296   Miles recorded *In A Silent Way* on February 18, 1969.

297   Miles recorded *Bitches Brew* from August 19-21, 1969, and on January 28, 1970.

302   Miles Davis met Richard Pryor for the first time. Miles hired Richard to open for some of his concerts, including at the Village Gate.

303   Miles Davis met Bill Cosby at Chicago O'Hare International Airport.

304   It's found out by Miles that his wife Betty is sleeping with Jimi Hendrix.

305   Miles and Betty get divorced in 1969.

Around this time, Miles began seeing two other women, Marguerite Eskridge and Jackie Battle.

306   Marguerite later became the mother of Miles' youngest son Erin.

CHAPTER 15

311   From 1969 into the next four years, Miles completed ten albums including *In A Silent Way, Bitches Brew, Miles Davis Sextet: At Fillmore West, Miles Davis: At Fillmore, Miles Davis Septet: At the Isle of Wight, Live-Evil, Miles Davis Septet: At Philharmonic Hall, On the Corner, Big Fun*, and *Get Up With It*.

Saxophonist Steve Grossman replaced Wayne Shorter after Wayne quit the band in fall 1969.

312   Miles added percussionist Airto Moreira to the band.

313   Miles played on the televised 1970 Grammy Awards show.

Miles' son Gregory returned from Vietnam in 1970.

314   Miles recorded *A Tribute to Jack Johnson* soundtrack album to the movie on February 18 and April 7, 1970.

Miles wrote the *A Tribute to Jack Johnson* tunes when he was training at Gleason's Gym with Bobby McQuillen.

315   *A Tribute to Jack Johnson* was released on February 24, 1971, and Miles said the album received little promotion from Columbia if any at all.

317   Miles Davis toured with Santana as the opening act.

318   Miles played a Woodstock-esque concert in August 1970 at the Isle of Wight.

Miles Davis and Jimi Hendrix were scheduled to meet one another in London to discuss collaborating on an album. Their meeting was a missed connection, and Jimi died in London on September 18, 1970.

319   Miles was voted Jazzman of the Year and his band Band of the Year by *Down Beat* magazine in 1971.

321   Around this time, Miles was making $100,000 a year plus royalties.

Miles met Sly Stone.

322   Miles recorded *On the Corner* between June 1-6 and on July 7, 1972.

323   Miles upgraded all his musical equipment to electric in 1973.

Miles began using a microphone amplifier connected to his trumpet.

325   In 1971, Miles had a gallstone operation.

Miles broke up with Marguerite Eskridge.

326   Marguerite became pregnant with Miles' son Erin.

327   Miles crashed his Lamborghini and broke both of his ankles after falling asleep at the wheel on October 19, 1972.

328   Jackie Battle broke up with Miles Davis for good.

On the Corner was released by Columbia on October 11, 1972, and is one of Miles' worst-selling recordings. Miles said the album was made for young black kids, but

Columbia marketed it to the wrong demographic by promoting it on jazz radio stations to old white people when it should have been on R&B and rock stations.

330   Miles began contemplating retiring from music in 1974.

Miles Davis toured the US with Herbie Hancock's, band playing as the opening act for Herbie.

331   Irene, the mother of Miles' children, showed up at a party after a concert in St. Louis and began badmouthing Miles about her disappointments in him being a failure of a father and for their children growing up to be disappointments. She put a lot of blame on Miles, and Miles accepted it, knowing that she was speaking the truth.

In the summer of 1975, Miles thought again deeply about retiring from music due to drugs, illnesses, and personal troubles.

Miles finally quit after playing at Newport in 1975, primarily due to his health.

332   It would take Miles nearly six years to get back into music again.

CHAPTER 16

335   Miles entered a five year period of darkness that didn't involve music, only sex, cocaine, heroin, pills (Percodan and Seconal), and alcohol (Heinekens and cognac).

337   Marguerite Eskridge had Miles jailed in 1978 for non-support of their son Erin.

338   Drugs were making Miles Davis go insane. After hallucinating, Miles slapped a woman on the elevator, and she called the police on him. He was sent for a few days to a psych ward in Roosevelt Hospital.

339   George Butler, who used to work for Blue Note, became a producer over at Columbia Records around 1978 and tried to persuade Miles to return to music again.

340 Cicely Tyson came back into Miles Davis' life again and started taking care of him. She helped him to get off cocaine slowly and saw to it he was eating healthier and taking care of himself better. She helped him also to stop smoking.

341 Miles decided to return to music in 1980 and had gotten off drugs.

CHAPTER 17

343 Miles' first album made after returning to music was *The Man with the Horn*. Some of the tunes featured Miles' nephew Vincent Wilburn on drums.

345 Bill Evans died on September 15, 1980, from a bleeding ulcer, cirrhosis of the liver, and bronchial pneumonia.

Charlie Mingus died the year before Bill on January 5, 1979.

346 Miles bought a new yellow 308 GTSI Ferrari sports coupe.

347 *The Man with the Horn* was released in July 1981 to not so favorable reviews from the critics but sold well.

348 Miles Davis and Cicely Tyson married on Thanksgiving Day 1981 at Bill Cosby's house in Massachusetts.

352 Miles began sketching a lot after Cicely bought him some sketchpads. Later sketching and painting would become a new professional artistic output for Miles on par with his music.

353 Prince became a significant influence on Miles Davis musically after Miles heard him for the first time in 1982.

Miles recorded the live album *We Want Miles* on June 27, July 5 & October 4, 1981.

354 Miles recorded the studio album *Star People* between August 11, 1982, and February 3, 1983.

355 Miles Davis met Willie Nelson and his wife Connie in Las Vegas, Nevada, and became good friends.

357 *We Want Miles* won a Grammy in 1982 for Best Jazz Instrumental Performance by a Soloist.

51

Miles was named Jazz Musician of the Year in *Jazz Forum: the Magazine of the International Jazz Federation.*

Miles began recording *Decoy* on June 30, 1983.

CHAPTER 18

358   Columbia Records & The Black Music Association organized a celebration for Miles Davis on November 6, 1983, at Radio City Music Hall called "Miles Ahead: A Tribute to an American Music Legend." Bill Cosby hosted, and it featured many famous jazz musicians including many members from Miles' old bands such as Herbie Hancock, Ron Carter, Jackie McLean, among many others.

359   Miles Davis' nephew Vincent Wilburn joined Miles' working band in 1985.

Miles won the Sonning Music Award for lifetime achievement in music in Denmark in November 1984.

361   Miles recorded his final album for Columbia titled *You're Under Arrest* from January 26, 1984, to January 10, 1985.

362   Miles left Columbia and signed with Warner Bros in 1985. Warner Bros. would keep all of Miles Davis' music's rights, so Miles had others compose the tunes on the albums.

365   Miles Davis moved into Cicely Tyson's apartment on Fifth Avenue.

370   Miles began recording *Tutu*, his first album for Warner Bros., on February 6, 1986. Marcus Miller wrote most of the music on the album.

373   Miles Davis heard and met guitarist Joseph Foley McCreary aka "Foley" for the first time, and brought him into the band.

374   In 1986 and 1987, Miles composed the musical score for the Christopher Reeve & Morgan Freeman film *Street Smart.* The film was released in theaters on March 20, 1987, by The Cannon Group. The soundtrack is still unreleased.

In 1986 a legendary standoff happened between Miles Davis and trumpeter Wynton Marsalis at the inaugural Vancouver International Jazz Festival in Vancouver, Canada. As Miles played live on stage, Wynton walked on uninvited and unannounced and tried to sit in with Miles' band. He said in Miles' ear, "They told me to come up here." Miles became infuriated and told him, "Man, get the fuck off the stage." This incident would later set the scene for one of jazz history's most controversial and heated debates.

375   Miles Davis appeared on Season 2 Episode 6 of *Miami Vice*. The episode titled "Junk Love" had Miles playing a pimp name Ivory Jones. The episode aired on November 8, 1985.

376   Miles starred in a famous Honda scooter commercial in 1984 that gained him a lot of recognition.

CHAPTER 19

382   Miles Davis and Marcus Miller began composing the musical score for the film *Siesta*. The recording was from January to February 1987.

383   Miles Davis let his nephew Vincent Wilburn go from the band in March 1987 because he dropped time as the drummer.

386   Miles Davis' best friend Gil Evans passed away on March 20, 1988, in Cuernavaca, Mexico, from peritonitis.

387   Miles Davis was knighted on November 13, 1988, and inducted into the Knights of Malta.

388   Miles' third Warner Bros. album *Amandla* was released on May 18, 1989.

389   The unreleased Columbia album *Aura* was released in 1989.

Miles began doing exhibitions of his paintings and was selling them as well.

391   Miles' divorce with Cicely Tyson was finalized in 1989.

MILES DAVIS AUDIO INTERVIEWS

Title: Miles Davis 1953 Interview with DJ Harry Frost on KXLW, East St. Louis
   Date: July or August, 1953, in St. Louis, Missouri
   Interviewer: Harry Frost
   Available On YouTube: https://www.youtube.com/watch?v=5CvG3jEGr9w
   Originally Aired On: Show: Fresh Air | Radio Station: KXLW

Title: Miles Davis 1969 Interview with Swing Journal Magazine (Japan)
   Date: August 4, 1969, at Miles Davis' Home, 312 West 77th Street, New York
   Interviewer: Journalists for Swing Journal (Japan)
   Available On YouTube: http://www.youtube.com/watch?v=EpYNZi2S0m4

Title: Miles Davis 1980 Interview with Kishore Manwar on KWMU-FM, St. Louis
   Date: August 3, 1980, in St. Louis, Missouri
   Interviewer: Kishore Manwar
   Available On YouTube: https://www.youtube.com/watch?v=Qf97bvkiATA
   Originally Aired On: Show: Miles Beyond | Radio Network: KWMU-FM

Title: Talking Jazz with Ben Sidran, Episode 1:Miles Davis
   Date: January 30, 1986, in Malibu, California
   Interviewer: Ben Sidran
   Available Online: https://www.youtube.com/watch?v=T3HpWUJOSGs
   Originally Aired On: Show: Sidran On Record | Radio Network: NPR

MILES DAVIS VIDEO INTERVIEWS

Title: Miles Davis interview, 1982
  Date: 1982, in NBC Studio 8G RCA Building, 30 Rockefeller Plaza, New York
  Interviewer: Bryant Gumbel
  Available On YouTube:
  http://www.youtube.com/watch?v=IHeYG9SNaS0
  Originally Aired On: TV Network NBC (National Broadcasting Company)

Title: Miles Davis Interview 1984 Part I
  Date: 1984, in Europe
  Interviewer: N/A
  Available On YouTube:
  Part I: http://www.youtube.com/watch?v=51WOgwMmHcE
  Part II: http://www.youtube.com/watch?v=ker7wG5fG2w
  Part III: http://www.youtube.com/watch?v=gdKa4Pks0X8

Title: Miles Davis Aura pt.1
  Original Title: Days With Miles Davis
  Date: January 31-February 4, 1985, in Denmark
  Available On YouTube:
  Part 1: http://www.youtube.com/watch?v=8I_oC4KJu-M
  Part 2: http://www.youtube.com/watch?v=PvQcCfpa9EA
  Part 3: http://www.youtube.com/watch?v=HBM5HcVaumU
  Part 4: http://www.youtube.com/watch?v=aOK7nrpQNNE
  Originally Aired On: Danmarks Radio/TV

Title: ど緊張 Interviews : MILES DAVIS 1985/08/16
  Original Title: マイルスのトランペットは泣いている (Miles Trumpet is Crying)
  Date: August 16, 1985, in Tokyo, Japan
  Interviewer: Tamori
  Available On YouTube:
  http://www.youtube.com/watch?v=Hhnb215rkrE
  Originally Aired On: N/A

Title: Miles Davis TV Interview 1986
  Date: 1986, in Philadelphia
  Interviewer: Bill Boggs
  Available Online:
  http://www.billboggs.com/miles_vid.htm
  Originally Aired On: Show: Time Out | TV Network: Channel 3 KYW-TV

Title: Miles Ahead: The Music of Miles Davis
  Date: October 8, 1986
  Interviewer: N/A
  Available On YouTube:
  https://vimeo.com/13967790
  Original Aired On: Show: Great Performances | TV Network: PBS

Title: Miles Davis Documentary Part I
Original Title: Miles Noir Sur Blanc
Date: Circa November 4, 1986, in Paris, France
Interviewer: N/A
Available On YouTube:
Part I: http://www.youtube.com/watch?v=JxjGnyUSa14
Part II: http://www.youtube.com/watch?v=t9I085yc87g
Part III: http://www.youtube.com/watch?v=hbPsfSe-P9E
Originally Aired On: N/A

Title: Miles Davis - The Tube Interview 1986
Date: November 14, 1986, in Newcastle upon Tyne, England, UK
Interviewer: Jools Holland
Available Online:
http://www.muzu.tv/thetube/miles-davis-the-tube-interview-1986-music-video/27798?country=ww&locale=en
Originally Aired On: Show: The Tube | TV Network: Channel 4

Title: Miles Davis Interview On His Art And Paintings Part 1 June 29, 1988.wmv
Date: June 29, 1988, in Toronto, Ontario, Canada
Interviewer: Laurie Brown
Available On YouTube:
Part 1: http://www.youtube.com/watch?v=Aplp6pPVvCg
Part 2: http://www.youtube.com/watch?v=qDkdLCbVJGo
Originally Aired On: Show: The NewMusic | TV Network: City TV

Title: Rare Interview With Miles Davis
Date: Circa July 10, 1988, in Munich, Germany
Interviewer: N/A
Available On DVD: Miles Davis: Live In Munich
Studio: Pioneer

Title: The Arsenio Hall Show
Date: June 14, 1989, in Stage 29 Paramount Studios, Hollywood, California
Interviewer: Arsenio Hall
Available On: N/A
Originally Aired On: Show: The Arsenio Hall Show | TV Network: CBS

Title: 11/12/89: Miles Davis
Date: November 12, 1989, in New York
Interviewer: Harry Reasoner
Available On CBSNews.com: 11/12/89: Miles Davis (Short 1:37 Min Clip)
        http://www.cbsnews.com/video/watch/?id=4599512n
Available Online (Full Version):
Part 1 http://www.rbgtube.com/play.php?vid=3536
Part 2 http://www.rbgtube.com/play.php?vid=3535
Originally Aired On: Show: 60 Minutes | TV Network: CBS

Title: Miles Davis, deux mots, quatre paroles
Date: Circa Mid 1980's
Interviewer: Realisateurs: Jean-Pierre Krief / Michel Reinette

56

Available On YouTube: http://www.youtube.com/watch?v=llDPkFcAAck

Title: I Remember Miles-Part 1
    Date: Circa Mid-Late 1980's
    Interviewer: Mal Adams
    Available On DVD: Japan-Based DVD "I Remember Miles"
    Available On YouTube:
    Part 1: http://www.youtube.com/watch?v=nMWXBEj4HoE
    Part 2: http://www.youtube.com/watch?v=TspkkqLP3Bs
    Part 3: http://www.youtube.com/watch?v=r7Sq3wQTKPU
    Part 4: http://www.youtube.com/watch?v=2ph8WedhtQM
    Studio: Totown Digital Media

MILES ON BLU-RAY & DVD

Blu-Ray Title: Miles Ahead (Motion Picture)

Released on July 19, 2016

Studio: Sony Pictures Classics/Sony Pictures Home Entertainment

Blu-Ray Title: Miles Davis: Live At Montreux 1991

Released on March 19, 2013

Studio: Eagle Rock Entertainment

Blue-Ray Title: Miles Davis Birth of the Cool

Blu-Ray Content: Disc 1: Documentary, Disc 2: Live From Montreux

Released on February 25, 2020

Studio: Eagle Rock Entertainment

DVD Title: The Miles Davis Story

DVD Content: Documentary

Released on November 26, 2002

Studio: Sony Legacy

DVD Title: Miles Davis: The Cool Jazz Sound

DVD Content: Miles Davis on "The Robert Herridge Theater"

Recorded April 2, 1959 at Studio 61 in New York City

Studio: EFOR FILMS

DVD Title: Miles Davis: So What (Same as above plus one additional concert)

DVD Content: Miles Davis on "The Robert Herridge Theater"

Recorded April 2, 1959 at Studio 61 in New York City

Recorded November 7, 1967 in Karlsruhe, Germany

Studio: Salt Peanuts

DVD Title: Miles Davis Quintet: Milan 1964

Recorded October 11, 1964 at Teatro Dell'Arte in Milano, Italy

Studio: Impro-Jazz Spain

DVD Title: Miles Davis Quintet: European Tour 1967

Recorded October 31, 1967 in Stockholm, Sweden

Recorded November 7, 1967 in Karlsruhe, Germany

Studio: Impro-Jazz

DVD Title: Miles Davis: Around Midnight (Same as above concert)

    Recorded October 31, 1967 in Stockholm, Sweden

    Recorded November 7, 1967 in Karlsruhe, Germany

    Studio: Salt Peanuts

DVD Title: Miles Davis Quintet: Live in Copenhagen & Rome 1969

    Recorded November 4, 1969 at Tivoli Koncertsal in Copenhagen, Denmark

    Recorded October 27, 1969 at Teatro Sistine in Rome, Italy

    Studio: Jazz Shots Spain

DVD Title: Miles Davis Quintet: The 1969 Berlin Concert

    Recorded November 7, 1969 at Berlin Philharmonie in Berlin Germany

    Studio: Jazz Shots Spain

DVD Title: Miles Davis: Miles Electric: A Different Kind of Blue

    Recorded August 29, 1970 at the Isle of Wight Festival in England

    Studio: Eagle Rock Entertainment

DVD Title: Miles Davis & Keith Jarrett: The 1971 Berlin Concert

    Recorded November 6, 1971 at Berliner Philharmonie in Berlin, Germany

    Studio: Jazz VIP

DVD Title: Miles Davis Septet: Live in Stockholm 1973

    Recorded October 27, 1973 in Stockholm, Sweden

    Studio: Rare Jazz Footage

DVD Title: Miles Davis: Stadthalle, Vienna 1973

    Recorded November 3, 1973

    Studio: Jazz VIP

DVD Title: Miles Davis Septet: Live in Poland 1983

    Recorded October 23, 1983 at Congress Hall in Warsaw, Poland

    Studio: Jazz Shots Spain

DVD Title: Miles Davis: Live in Montreal

    Recorded June 28, 1985 at Montreal Jazz Festival in Montreal, Canada

    Studio: Pioneer

DVD Title: Miles Davis: That's What Happened: Live in Germany 1987

    Recorded July 18, 1987 at Gasteig Philharmonie Concert Hall in Munich, Germany

    Studio: Eagle Rock Entertainment

DVD Title: Miles Davis: Live in Munich (Two disc)

Recorded July 10, 1988 at Gasteig Philharmonie Concert Hall in Munich, Germany

Studio: Pioneer

DVD Title: Miles Davis: Time After Time: Live at the Philharmonic Concert Hall: Complete Edition (Same as above concert w/1 disc)

Recorded July 10, 1988 at Gasteig Philharmonie Concert Hall in Munich, Germany

Studio: Standing Oh!vation

(My recommendation, don't buy this version)

DVD Title: Miles Davis: Live in Germany 1988 (Same as above two DVDs w/1 disc)

Recorded July 10, 1988 at Gasteig Philharmonie Concert Hall in Munich, Germany

Studio: Immortal

(My recommendation, don't buy this version)

DVD Title: Miles Davis: Live in Paris

Recorded November 3, 1989 at the 10th Paris Jazz Festival Zenith Paris, France

Studio: Warner Bros.

DVD Title: Miles Davis Collector's Edition

Containing the two released DVDs from Eagle Rock Entertainment in a boxset (Miles Electric & Live in Germany)

Studio: Eagle Rock Entertainment

BUYERS GUIDE: MILES DAVIS COLLECTOR'S CD APPRAISAL

In this section I am going to personally appraise Miles Davis' CDs that are sold as special edition packages, maybe a limited run, rare, imported, and currently out of print CDs new and used. I don't believe anyone to have ever done this before so I am establishing the market standard prices myself for these items based on an extensive study of the current prices aggregated. This appraisal guide is current as of March 2011. Prices are subject to change.

*New – The Current Retail Price As In Stores & Online Currently
*MC – Second Hand Owned Factory Sealed & Mint Condition Items
NM – Near Mint Condition
A – Average
BA – Below Average
P – Poor

The quality reflects the overall quality of the item based on any packaging (metal, plastic, etc.), the disc quality, CD booklet/liner notes, books, and all extra accessories or special items that maybe included in the package. As a buyer of a product you really want to stay away from purchasing most all used BA & P rated items unless possibly it is something that is extremely old or rare.

*The prices for new, factory sealed, and mint condition items should roughly be about the same price whether you are buying or selling.

CONCERT CDS

1948-1949 The Complete Birth of the Cool (Contains Live at the Royal Roost 1948) [Label: Blue Note] (1998)
New: $11.68   NM: $8.00   A: $6.00   BA: $2.00   P: $0.20

1949 The Miles Davis/Tadd Dameron Quintet In Paris Festival International Dejazz May, 1949 [Label: Sony Japan] (2009)
New: $31.47   NM: $24.00   A: $18.00   BA: $6.00   P: $0.60

1950 Birdland Jam Session: June 30, 1950 [Label: RLR Records] (2009)
New: $15.87   NM: $12.00   A: $9.00   BA: $3.00   P: $0.30

1951 Birdland 1951 [Label: Blue Note] (2004)
New: $11.84   NM: $8.00   A: $6.00   BA: $2.00   P: $0.20

1958 Miles Davis at Newport 1958 [Label: Columbia] (2008)
New: $8.70   NM: $6.00   A: $4.50   BA: $1.50   P: $0.15

1960 Miles Davis In Stockholm 1960 Complete With John Coltrane and Sonny Stitt [Label: DIW] (1992)
New: $70,93   NM: $56.00   A: $42.00   BA: $14.00   P: $1.40

1961 Miles Davis in Person Friday and Saturday Nights at the Blackhawk, Complete [Label: Columbia] (2003)
New: $27.84   NM: $24.00   A: $18.00   BA: $6.00   P: $0.60

1961 Miles Davis at Carnegie Hall [Label: Columbia] (1998)
New: $16.31   NM: $12.00   A: $9.00   BA: $3.00   P: $0.30

1963 Live at the 1963 Monterey Jazz Festival [Label: Monterey Jazz Festival] (2007)
New: $11.98   NM: $8.00   A: $6.00   BA: $2.00   P: $0.20

1963 Miles in Europe [Label: Columbia] (2008)
New: $6.10   NM: $4.00   A: $3.00   BA: $1.00   P: $0.10

1964 My Funny Valentine: Miles Davis in Concert [Label: Columbia] (2005)
New: $7.91   NM: $6.00   A: $4.50   BA: $1.50   P: $0.15

1964 'Four' & More: Recorded Live in Concert [Label: Columbia] (2005)
New: $9.68   NM: $8.00   A: $6.00   BA: $2.00   P: $0.20

1964 Miles Davis The Complete Concert 1964 My Funny Valentine + Four & More
[Label: Columbia] (1992)
MC: $80.00   NM: $64.00   A: $48.00   BA: $16.00   P: $1.60

1964 Miles in Berlin
[Label: Columbia] (2005)
New: $8.47   NM: $6.00   A: $4.50   BA: $1.50   P: $0.15

1964 Miles in Tokyo
[Label: Columbia] (2008)
New: $8.72   NM: $6.00   A: $4.50   BA: $1.50   P: $0.15

1964 Miles Davis Quintet The Unissued Japanese Concerts
[Label: Domino] (2011)
New: $20.00   NM: $16.00   A: $12.00   BA: $4.00   P: $0.40

1964 Miles Davis The Complete Copenhagen Concert 1964 (Out of Print)
[Label: Magnetic] (N/A)
MC: $50.00   NM: $40.00   A: $30.00   BA: $10.00   P: $1.00

1964 Sindelfingen 1964
[Label: Mega Disc] (N/A)
MC: $50.00   NM: $40.00   A: $30.00   BA: $10.00   P: $1.00

1964 Davisiana (Out of Print)
[Label: Moon] (1993)
MC: $50.00   NM: $40.00   A: $30.00   BA: $10.00   P: $1.00

1966 Miles Davis Quintet Live At The Oriental Theatre 1966
[Label: Sunburn] (2010)
New: $40.00   NM: $32.00   A: $24.00   BA: $8.00   P: $0.80

1966-1967 Live At Newport 1966-1967
[Label: Domino Jazz] (2010)
MC: $17.32   NM: $14.00   A: $10.50   BA: $3.50   P: $0.35

1967 Winter in Europe 1967
[Label: Gambit Spain] (2010)
New: $16.44   NM: $12.00   A: $9.00   BA: $3.00   P: $0.30

1969 Complete Live at the Blue Coronet 1969
[Label: Domino Jazz] (2010)
New: $22.13   NM: $16.00   A: $12.00   BA: $4.00   P: $0.40

1969 1969 Miles: Festiva De Juan Pins
[Label: Sony Japan] (1993)
New: $35.00   NM: $28.00   A: $21.00   BA: $7.00   P: $0.70

1969 Live in Rome & Copenhagen 1969
[Label: Gambit Spain] (2010)
New: $14.19   NM: $12.00   A: $9.00   BA: $3.00   P: $0.30

1969 Live in Berlin 1969
[Label: Gambit Spain] (2010)
New: $14.09   NM: $12.00   A: $9.00   BA: $3.00   P: $0.30

1970 Black Beauty: Miles Davis at Fillmore West
[Label: Columbia] (1997)
New: $29.95   NM: $24.00   A: $18.00   BA: $6.00   P: $0.60

1970 Miles Davis At Fillmore
[Label: Columbia] (1997)
New: $14.07   NM: $10.00   A: $7.50   BA: $2.50   P: $0.25

1970 Live at the Fillmore East (March 7, 1970) It's About That Time
[Label: Columbia] (2000)
New: $14.58   NM: $12.00   A: $9.00   BA: $3.00   P: $0.30

1970 Bitches Brew Live
[Label: Columbia] (2011)
New: $15.50   NM: $12.00   A: $9.00   BA: $3.00   P: $0.30

1972 Miles Davis in Concert: Recorded Live at Philharmonic Hall, New York
[Label: Columbia] (1997)
New: $16.77   NM: $14.00   A: $10.50   BA: $3.50   P: $0.35

1973-1991 The Complete Miles Davis At Montreux: 1973-1991
[Label: Columbia] (2002)
New: $428.95   NM: $320.00   A: $240.00   BA: $80.00   P: $8.00

1973 Live in Vienna 1973
[Label: Gambit Spain] (2009)
New: $16.14   NM: $12.00   A: $9.00   BA: $3.00   P: $0.30

1974 Dark Magus
[Label: Columbia] (1997)
New: $15.01   NM: $12.00   A: $9.00   BA: $3.00   P: $0.30

1975 Agharta
[Label: Columbia] (1997)
New: $13.39   NM: $10.00   A: $7.50   BA: $2.50   P: $0.25

1975 Pangaea
[Label: Columbia] (1997)
New: $14.72   NM: $12.00   A: $9.00   BA: $3.00   P: $0.30

1981 We Want Miles
[Label: Columbia Europe] (1992)
New: $11.79   NM: $8.00   A: $6.00   BA: $2.00   P: $0.20

1981 Live at the Hollywood Bowl 1981
[Label: Gambit Spain] (2010)
New: $12.31   NM: $10.00   A: $7.50   BA: $2.50   P: $0.25

64

1983 Live in Poland 1983
[Label: Gambit Spain] (2008)
New: $18.58   NM: $14.00   A: $10.50   BA: $3.50   P: $0.35

1983 Warsaw Concert 1983
[Label: Immortal] (2010)
New: $15.64   NM: $12.00   A: $9.00   BA: $3.00   P: $0.30

1988 Miles Davis Munich Concert
[Label: Deluxe] (2005)
New: $18.02   NM: $14.00   A: $10.50   BA: $3.50   P: $0.35

1988 Avignon: The Last Concert
[Label: Performance] (2008)
MC: $50.00   NM: $40.00   A: $30.00   BA: $10.00   P: $1.00

1988-1991 Live Around The World
[Label: Warner Bros.] (1996)
New: $8.68   NM: $8.00   A: $6.00   BA: $2.00   P: $0.20

1991 Miles & Quincy Live At Montreux
[Label: Warner Bros.] (1993)
New: $10.41   NM: $8.00   A: $6.00   BA: $2.00   P: $0.20

OWN MILES DAVIS CDS ON A BUDGET

All Miles: The Prestige Albums [14 Disc]
[Label: Prestige] [Cat #: 5321756] (2010)
New: $92.44   NM: $80.00   A: $60.00   BA: $20.00   P: $2.00

The Legendary Prestige Quintet Sessions, Miles Davis Quintet [4 Disc]
[Label: Prestige] [Cat #: PRCD4-4444-2] (2006)
New: $37.05   NM: $29.00   A: $21.00   BA: $ 7.00   P: $0.70

The Best of Miles Davis: The Capitol/Blue Note Years
[Label: Blue Note] [Cat #: D111000] (1992)
New: $11.55   NM: $8.00   A: $6.00   BA: $2.00   P: $0.20

Birdland 1951
[Label: Blue Note] [Cat #: 41779] (2004)
New: $11.84   NM: $8.00   A: $6.00   BA: $2.00   P: $0.20

Miles Davis, The Complete Columbia Album Collection
[Label: Legacy] [Cat #: 88697 55852 2] (2010)
New: $265.30   NM: $200.00   A: $150.00   BA: $50.00   P: $5.00

Tutu
[Label: Warner Bros.] [Cat #: 2-25490] (1986)
New: $7.98   NM: $5.00   A: $4.00   BA: $2.00   P: $0.20

Amandla
[Label: Warner Bros.] [Cat #: 2-25873] (1989)
New: $12.98   NM: $8.00   A: $6.00   BA: $2.00   P: $0.20

Music From Siesta
[Label: Warner Bros.] [Cat #: 2-25655] (1987)
New: $8.96   NM: $8.00   A: $6.00   BA: $2.00   P: $0.20

Dingo
[Label: Warner Bros.] [Cat #: 2-26438] (1991)
New: $13.76   NM: $12.00   A: $9.00   BA: $3.00   P: $0.30

Doo-Bop
[Label: Warner Bros.] [Cat #: 2-26938] (1992)
New: $7.98   NM: $5.00   A: $4.00   BA: $2.00   P: $0.20

Live Around The World
[Label: Warner Bros. Europe] [Cat #: 9362 46032-2] (1996)
New: $8.68   NM: $8.00   A: $6.00   BA: $2.00   P: $0.20

Miles & Quincy Live At Montreux
[Label: Warner Bros.] (1993)
New: $10.41   NM: $8.00   A: $6.00   BA: $2.00   P: $0.20

OWN MILES DAVIS HIGHEST QUALITY CDS: NO BUDGET

Cookin' With the Miles Davis Quintet (24 Karat Gold Disc) (Out of print)
[Label: DCC] [Cat #: GZS 1044] (1993) Mastered by Steve Hoffman
MC: $100.00   NM: $80.00   A: $60.00   BA: $20.00   P: $2.00

Relaxin' With the Miles Davis Quintet (24 Karat Gold Disc) (Out of print)
[Label: DCC] [Cat #: GZS 1052] (1994) Mastered by Steve Hoffman
MC: $100.00   NM: $80.00   A: $60.00   BA: $20.00   P: $2.00

Workin' With the Miles Davis Quintet (24 Karat Gold Disc) (Out of print)
[Label: DCC] [Cat #: GZS 1063] (1994) Mastered by Steve Hoffman
MC: $100.00   NM: $80.00   A: $60.00   BA: $20.00   P: $2.00

Steamin' With the Miles Davis Quintet (24 Karat Gold Disc) (Out of print)
[Label: DCC] [Cat #: GZS 1065] (1994) Mastered by Steve Hoffman
MC: $100.00   NM: $80.00   A: $60.00   BA: $20.00   P: $2.00

Miles Davis, The New Miles Davis Quintet (24 Karat Gold Disc) (Out of print)
[Label: DCC] [Cat #: GZS 1100] (1996) Mastered by Steve Hoffman
MC: $100.00   NM: $80.00   A: $60.00   BA: $20.00   P: $2.00

Miles Davis, The Musings of Miles (24 Karat Gold Disc) (Out of print)
[Label: DCC] [Cat #: GZS 1106] (1997) Mastered by Steve Hoffman
MC: $100.00   NM: $80.00   A: $60.00   BA: $20.00   P: $2.00

Miles Davis and Milt Jackson, Quintet/Sextet (24 Karat Gold Disc) (Out of print)
[Label: DCC] [Cat #: GZS 1113] (1997) Mastered by Steve Hoffman
MC: $100.00   NM: $80.00   A: $60.00   BA: $20.00   P: $2.00

Chronicles – The Complete Prestige Recordings 1951-1956
[Cat #: 8PRCD-012-2] [8 Disc] (1993)
New: $124.98   NM: $100.00   A: $70.00   BA: $25.00   P: $2.50

The Blue Note and Capitol Recordings (Out of Print)
[Label: Blue Note] [Cat #: CDP 7243 8 27475 2 9] (1993)
MC: $50.00   NM: $40.00   A: $30.00   BA: $10.00   P: $1.00

Miles Davis, Vol. 1
[Label: Blue Note] [Cat #: 32610] (2001)
New: $11.19   NM: $8.00   A: $6.00   BA: $2.00   P: $0.20

Miles Davis, Vol. 2
[Label: Blue Note] [Cat #: 32611] (2001)
New: $11.19   NM: $8.00   A: $6.00   BA: $2.00   P: $0.20

Miles Davis, Vol. 3
[Label: Blue Note] [Cat #: BCD-0051]
MC: $50.00   NM: $40.00   A: $30.00   BA: $10.00   P: $1.00

67

Birdland 1951
[Label: Blue Note] [Cat #: 41779] (2004)
New: $11.84   NM: $8.00   A: $6.00   BA: $2.00   P: $0.20
The Complete Live at the Plugged Nickel 1965 [8 CD Boxset] (Out of print)
[Label: Legacy] [Cat #: CXK 66955] (1995)
MC: $300.00   NM: $240.00   A: $180.00   BA: $60.00   P: $6.00

Genius of Miles Davis
1 x Trumpet /Carrying Case, 8 x Box Sets, 1 x T-Shirt, 1 x Lithograph, 1 x Mouthpiece
Limited Edition 1,955 Units [8 Box Sets]
[Label: Legacy] (2010)
New: $749.00   NM: $650.00   A: $500.00   BA: N/A   P: $ N/A

Sketches of Spain (50th Anniversary Enhanced 2 CD Legacy Edition) [2 Disc]
[Label: Legacy] [Cat #: 88697439492] (2009)
New: $13.31   NM: $10.00   A: $7.50   BA: $2.50   P: $0.25

Bitches Brew: 40th Anniversary Collector's Edition [4 Disc]
4 x Disc, 2 x LPs, DVD, 48-Page 12x12 Book, Memorabilia Envelope, Large Poster
[Label: Legacy] [Cat #: 88697751502] (2010)
New: $93.55   NM: $72.00   A: $54.00   BA: $18.00   P: $1.80

Kind of Blue 50th Anniversary Collector's Edition [2 Disc]
2 x Disc, 180 Gram LP, DVD, 60-Page 12x12 Book, Memorabilia Envelope, Large Poster
[Label: Legacy] [Cat #: 88697335522] (2008)
New: $86.99   NM: $68.00   A: $51.00   BA: $17.00   P: $1.70

Tutu/Amandla/Doo-Bop [Box Set] (Out of Print)
[Label: Warner Bros.]
MC: $50.00   NM: $40.00   A: $30.00   BA: $10.00   P: $1.00

Siesta (SHM-CD)
[Label: Warner Music Japan] [Cat #: WPCR-13442] (2009)
New: $36.00   NM: $29.00   A: $21.00   BA: $ 7.00   P: $0.70

Dingo (Japan Paper Sleeve Mini LP CD)
[Label: Warner Music Japan] [Cat #: WPCR-12746] (2007) 24 Bit Remastered
New: $34.47   NM: $29.00   A: $21.00   BA: $ 7.00   P: $0.70

Live Around The World (SHM-CD)
[Label: Warner Music Japan] [Cat #: WPCR-13445] (2009)
New: $35.38   NM: $29.00   A: $21.00   BA: $ 7.00   P: $0.70

Miles & Quincy Live At Montreux (Paper Sleeve)
[Label: Warner Music Japan] [Cat #: WPCR-12749] (2007)
New: $10.41   NM: $8.00   A: $6.00   BA: $2.00   P: $0.20

BUYERS GUIDE: MILES DAVIS HIGH-RESOLUTION CDS

Some information on high-resolution disc formats and authoring processes.

Format	Applies to
Blu-Spec CD	Physical master creation (using a blue laser)
Blu-Spec CD2	Physical master creation (using a blue laser)
DSD	Audio mastering process
SACD	Optical audio disc format
Hybrid SACD	Red book layer and SACD layer optical audio disc formats
SHM-CD	Material used in manufacturing (transparent substrate)
DVD Audio	DVD audio disc format
HQCD	Material used in manufacturing (high-quality polycarbonate with silver alloy reflective layer)
UHQCD	CD manufacturing process/physical master creation (using photopolymer)
MQA-CD	A coding process that compresses a hi-res audio file for size that can be uncompressed back to a lossless audio file.

BLU-SPEC CDS

Blu-spec CD describes an Audio CD manufactured by a proprietary process introduced by Sony in late 2008. Its name derives from the similar manufacturing process to that used to create Blu-ray Discs. Instead of a traditional infra-red laser, a blue laser is used for recording the pits on the CD master that is needed for disc replication. The blue laser creates more precise pits, causing less distortion in the optical read-out process. A Blu-spec CD can be played on all CD players and does not require a blue laser to be read.

SONY/COLUMBIA MILES DAVIS BLU-SPEC CDS

1958 Miles [SICP-20075](2009.3.25)¥2,500
Agharta [SICP-20067~SICP-20068](2CD)(2009.2.18)¥3,500
A Tribute to Jack Johnson [SICP-20060](2009.2.18)¥2,500
Bitches Brew [SICP-20002~SICP-20003](2CD)(2008.12.24)¥3,500
E.S.P. [SICP-20057](2009.2.18)¥2,500
'Four' & More Recorded Live in Concert [SICP-20055](2009.2.18)¥2,500
Get Up With It [SICP-20065~SICP-20066](2CD)(2009.2.18)¥3,500
In A Silent Way [SICP-20059](2009.2.18)¥2,500
Kind of Blue [SICP-20001](2008.12.24)¥2,500
Live-Evil [SICP-20063~SICP-20064](2CD)(2009.2.18)¥3,500
Miles Ahead [SICP-20052](2009.2.18)¥2,500
Miles Davis at Fillmore: Live at the Fillmore East
    [SICP-20061~SICP-20062](2CD)(2009.2.18)¥3,500
Miles in Berlin [SICP-20080](2009.3.25)¥2,500
Miles in Europe [SICP-20079](2009.3.25)¥2,500
Miles in Tokyo [SICP-20056](2009.2.18)¥2,500
Miles Smiles [SICP-20058](2009.2.18)¥2,500
Milestones [SICP-20053](2009.2.18)¥2,500
My Funny Valentine Miles Davis in Concert [SICP-20006](2008.12.24)¥2,500
Nefertiti [SICP-20082](2009.3.25)¥2,500
On the Corner [SICP-20005](2008.12.24)¥2,500
Porgy and Bess [SICP-20076](2009.3.25)¥2,500
Pangaea [SICP-20069~SICP-20070](2CD)(2009.2.18)¥2,500
'Round About Midnight [SICP-20004](2008.12.24)¥2,500
Seven Steps to Heaven [SICP-20078](2009.3.25)¥2,500
Sketches of Spain [SICP-20054](2009.2.18)¥2,500
Someday My Prince Will Come [SICP-20077](2009)¥2,500
Sorcerer [SICP-20081](2009.3.25)¥2,500
The Man With the Horn [SICP-20083](2009.3.25)¥2,500
We Want Miles [SICP-20084~SICP-20085](2009.3.25)¥3,500
You're Under Arrest [SICP-20071](2009.2.18)¥2,500

BLU-SPEC CD2

Blu-spec CD2 – (The following is a direct translation from Japanese and may not read clearly) The following two improvements have been made to the Blu-spec CD manufacturing process.

1. A silicon wafer for semiconductor manufacturing was adopted as the master material. It enables finer processing than conventional glass and has the effect of creating highly accurate pits. Also, it was necessary to make a metal master for pressing with glass, but it will be possible to press directly on the master. For this reason, the step of introducing an error can be omitted.

2. A metal oxide resistor (thermal recording) was used for the recording layer of the master. Compared with the conventional photoresist (optical recording), there is an effect that pits with higher accuracy can be created.

SONY/COLUMBIA MILES DAVIS BLU-SPEC 2 CDS

Miles Davis *Masterpiece Collection Box* is a Blu-spec CD2 box set offering 24 full-length album reissues from Miles Davis on Columbia Records. (2013.10.9)¥51,040

Round About Midnight	Miles Davis
Miles Ahead	Sorcerer
Milestones	Nefertiti
1958 Miles	In A Silent Way
Porgy & Bess	Bitches Brew
Kind Of Blue	A Tribute To Jack Johnson
Sketches Of Spain	On The Corner
Someday My Prince Will Come	Get Up With It
My Funny Valentine	Agharta
Four & More	Pangaea
Miles In Berlin	The Man With The Horn
E.S.P.	You're Under Arrest

DSD SACD

Direct-Stream Digital (DSD) is the trademark name used by Sony and Philips for their system of recreating audible signals which uses pulse-density modulation encoding, a technology to store audio signals on digital storage media which is used for the Super Audio CD (SACD).

Super Audio CD (SACD) is a high-resolution, read-only optical audio disc format developed by Sony and Philips Electronics, the same companies that created the Compact Disc and the S/PDIF specification used in digital audio cables. SACD is designed to provide high-resolution audio in both stereo and surround sound modes.

SACD audio is stored in a format called Direct Stream Digital (DSD), which differs from the conventional PCM used by the compact disc or conventional computer audio systems.

DSD is 1-bit, has a sampling rate of 2.8224 MHz, and makes use of noise shaping quantization techniques in order to push 1-bit quantization noise up to inaudible ultrasonic frequencies. This gives the format a greater dynamic range and wider frequency response than the CD. The SACD format is capable of delivering a dynamic range of 120 dB from 20 Hz to 20 kHz and an extended frequency response up to 100 kHz, although most currently available players list an upper limit of 80–90 kHz and 20kHz is the upper limit of human hearing.

SONY/COLUMBIA MILES DAVIS DSD SACDS

A Tribute to Jack Johnson [SRGS-4504](1999.5.21)¥3,675
Bitches Brew [SIGP-20～SIGP-21](2CD)(2002.6.5)¥4,725
Cookin' [UCGO-9008](2011.1.26)¥4,800
E.S.P. [SRGS-4561](2000.10.12)¥3,675
Filles de Kilimanjaro [SIGP-13](2002.1.9)¥3,150
'Four' & More Recorded Live in Concert [SRGS-4529](2000.3.8)¥3,675
Friday Night Miles Davis in Person: At the Blackhawk, San Francisco Vol. 1
      [SRGS-4581](2001.4.11)¥3,150
Get Up With It [SIGP-22](2002.8.7)¥4,725
In A Silent Way (Multichannel/Surround Sound)[SIGP-29](2002.12.4)¥3,150
In A Silent Way (Original LP Mix From 1969)[SICP-10088](2007.10.24)¥2,730
Jazz at the Plaza: The Miles Davis Sextet Vol. 1 [SRGS-4586](2001.5.9)¥3,150
Kind of Blue [SRGS-4501](1999.5.21)¥3,675
Live-Evil [SIGP-24～SIGP-25](2CD)(2002.7.10)¥4,725
Miles Ahead [SRGS-4543](2000.6.7)¥3,675
Miles Smiles [SRGS-4538](2000.5.3)¥3,675
Milestones [SRGS-4585](2001.5.9)¥3,150
My Funny Valentine Miles Davis In Concert [SRGS-4503](1999.5.21)¥3,675
Nefertiti [SRGS-4521](1999.11.3)¥3,675
On The Corner [SRGS-4539](2000.5.3)¥3,675
Porgy and Bess [SRGS-4518](1999.9.8)¥3,675
Quiet Nights [SIGP-2](2001.10.24)¥3,150
'Round About Midnight [SRGS-4517](1999.9.8)¥3,675
Saturday Night Miles Davis in Person: At the Blackhawk, San Francisco Vol. 2
      [SRGS-4582](2001.4.11)¥3,150
Seven Steps To Heaven [SIGP-14](2002.2.6)¥3,150
Sketches of Spain [SRGS-4502](1999.5.21)¥3,675
Someday My Prince Will Come [SRGS-4544](2000.6.7)¥3,675
Sorcerer [SIGP-27](2002.9.4)¥3,150
The Man With the Horn [SRGS-4505](1999.5.21)¥3,675
You're Under Arrest [SRGS-4530](2000.3.8)¥3,675

HYBRID SACD

Hybrid **SACD** discs include a Red Book layer compatible with most ordinary Compact Disc players, dubbed the "CD layer," and a 4.7 GB SACD layer, dubbed the "HD layer."

SONY/COLUMBIA MILES DAVIS HYBRID SACDS

Bitches Brew [SICP-10089～SICP-10090](2CD)(2007.10.24)¥3,990
'Four' & More Recorded Live in Concert [SICP-10087](2007.10.24)¥2,730
In A Silent Way [SICP-10088](2007.10.24)¥2,730
Kind of Blue [SICP-10083](2007.10.24)¥2,730
Milestones [SICP-10082](2007.10.24)¥2,730
My Funny Valentine Miles Davis In Concert SICP-10086¥2,730
On The Corner [SICP-10091](2007.10.24)¥2,730
'Round About Midnight [SICP-10081](2007.10.24)¥2,730
Sketches of Spain [SICP-10084](2007.10.24)¥2,730
Someday My Prince Will Come [SICP-10085](2007.10.24)¥2,730

SACD/SHM

Cookin' [UCGO-9008](2011.1.26)¥4,500
Relaxin' [UCGO-9002](2010.8.25)¥4,500

SHM-CD

Super High Material CD (SHM-CD) is a CD manufacturing process that features enhanced audio quality through the use of a special polycarbonate plastic. Using a process developed by JVC and Universal Music Japan and discovered through the joint companies' research into LCD display manufacturing, SHM-CDs feature improved transparency on the data side of the disc, allowing for more accurate reading of CD data by the CD player laser head. SHM-CD format CDs are fully compatible with standard CD players.

PRESTIGE & WARNER BROS. SHM-CDS

Amandla [WPCR-13442](24 Bit Remastered)(2009.6.24)¥2,300
Ascenseur Pour L'echafaud (Lift to the Scaffold)
    [UCCU-9457](2008.5.28)¥2,800
Bags' Groove [UCCO-9651]
    (24 Bit Remastered)(2008.11.19)¥2,800
Bags' Groove [UCCO-9651](DSD Remastered)(2009.3.18)¥2,800
Collectors' Items [UCCO-9660](DSD Remastered)(2009.3.18)¥2,800
Cookin' [UCCO-9653](DSD Remastered)(2009.3.18)¥2,800
Dig [UCCO-9658](DSD Remastered)(2009.3.18)¥2,800
Doo-Bop [WPCR-134444](24 Bit Remastered)(2009.6.24)¥2,300
Live Around the World [WPCR-13445](24 Bit Remastered)(2009.6.24)¥2,300
Miles: The New Miles Davis Quintet [UCCO-9659](2009)¥2,800
Miles Davis and Milt Jackson Quintet/Sextet [UCCO-9661]
    (DSD Remastered)(2009.3.18)¥2,800
Miles Davis and the Modern Jazz Giants [UCCO-9504]
    (24 Bit Remastered)(2008.11.19)¥2,800
Miles Davis and the Modern Jazz Giants [UCCO-9504]
    (DSD Remastered)(2009.3.18)¥2,800
Music From Siesta [WPCR-13442](24 Bit Remastered)(2009.6.24)¥2,300
Relaxin' [UCCO-9652](DSD Remastered)(2009.3.18)¥2,800
Steamin' [UCCO-9655](DSD Remastered)(2009.3.18)¥2,800
The Musings of Miles [UCCO-9506](24 Bit Remastered)(2008.11.19)¥2,800
The Musings of Miles [UCCO-9662](DSD Remastered)(2009.3.18)¥2,800
Tutu [WPCR-13441](24 Bit Remastered)(2009.6.24)¥2,300
Walkin' [UCCO-9656](DSD Remastered)(2009.3.18)¥2,800

DVD-AUDIO

DVD-Audio (DVD-A) is a digital format for delivering high-fidelity audio content on a DVD. DVD-Audio is not intended to be a video delivery format and is not the same as video DVDs containing concert films or music videos.

DVD-Audio offers many possible configurations of audio channels, ranging from single-channel mono to 5.1-channel surround sound, at various sampling frequencies and sample rates.

Compared to the compact disc, the much higher capacity DVD format enables the inclusion of either:

- Considerably more music (with respect to total running time and quantity of songs) or
- Far higher audio quality, reflected by higher linear sampling rates and higher bit-per-sample resolution, and/or
- Additional channels for spatial sound reproduction.

Different bit depth/sampling rate/channel combinations can be used on a single disc. For instance, a DVD-Audio disc may contain a 96 kHz/24-bit 5.1-channel audio track as well as a 192 kHz/24-bit stereo audio track. Also, the channels of a track can be split into two groups stored at different resolutions. For example, the front speakers could be 96/24, while the surrounds are 48/20.

Audio is stored on the disc in Linear PCM format, which is either uncompressed or losslessly compressed with Meridian Lossless Packing. The maximum permissible total bit rate is 9.6 Megabits per second. Channel/resolution combinations that would exceed this need to be compressed. In uncompressed modes, it is possible to get up to 96/16 or 48/24 in 5.1, and 192/24 in stereo. To store 5.1 tracks in 88.2/20, 88.2/24, 96/20 or 96/24 MLP encoding is mandatory.

If no native stereo audio exists on the disc, the DVD-Audio player may be able to downmix the 5.1-channel audio to two-channel stereo audio if the listener does not have a surround sound setup (provided that the coefficients were set in the stream at authoring). Downmixing can only be done to two-channel stereo, not to other configurations, such as 4.0 quad. DVD-Audio may also feature menus, text subtitles, still images and video, plus in high end authoring systems it is also possible to link directly into a Video_TS folder that might contain video tracks, as well as PCM stereo and other "bonus" features.

WARNER BROS. DVD AUDIO

Tutu [9362-48429-9](5.1 Dolby Digital)(2002)$45.25

EMI/CAPITOL HQCD

Hi Quality CD (HQCD) utilizes a higher-quality polycarbonate in addition of adaptation of silver alloy as the reflective layer, so a Compact Disc with superior sound quality is realized. HQCD can be played on all Compact Disc players.

1) Use of higher-quality polycarbonate. Using Quality polycarbonate, which is used for LC TVs and plastic lens, high precision pit transcription can be achieved with this new material. The transparency and very low birefringence contribute to quality sound production.

2) Use of silver alloy as its reflective layer material. With its better reflectivity, sound, which is closer to its original master, is made possible.The alloy was originally developed for HDDVD, which was proposed as the next generation DVD.

CAPITOL JAZZ HQCD

Birth of the Cool [TOCJ-90013](2008)¥2,600

UHQCD

Ultimate High Quality CD (UHQCD). Conventional Audio CDs are produced using an injection molding technique to form "pits," representing audio source data on polycarbonate material. A photopolymer is used in this new method instead of polycarbonate to replicate a stamper's pits, making for very finely detailed pits.

Master Quality Authenticated CD (MQA-CD). MQA's captures and authenticates the sound of the original master recording by compressing it into a smaller file, and unpackages it with a decoder to turn it back into lossless file.

UNIVERSAL MUSIC JAPAN MQA/UHQCD

Relaxin' With The Miles Davis Quintet [UCCO-40036](2018)¥3,300

HARSH REALITIES

MILES DAVIS vs. WYNTON MARSALIS
A Criticism Piece

INTRODUCTION

I wrote this article initially for *Down Beat* magazine circa November 2, 2010, as I was nearing the end of writing my Miles Davis companion guide. The item was never associated with or tied to this book. I tried to get it solicited by going through the proper channels and having an editor look at it. Unfortunately, they didn't want to be bothered with it and turned me down before I could even send them the file. My original plan was to start at the top and take it down the list of jazz publications until I found a publisher. Instead, after the first rejection by *Down Beat*, I scrapped that idea and opted for a better one. Since I was writing it simultaneously, I thought, why not put it in my book?

I felt compelled to write this article because I think it is something that people who listen to jazz music need to contemplate. I want to get the wheels of your brain in motion and have those cogs turning. You have the right to disagree with what I have to say; we are all entitled to our opinions. Though, I believe there is a consensus among half, if not the majority, of jazz listeners who disagree with Wynton Marsalis and his standpoint on jazz.

Occasionally I browse the Internet through Google searches and jazz forums looking for other people's opinions on either Wynton Marsalis (stand-alone) or Miles Davis vs. Wynton Marsalis. My observation is that there truly is a great divide, and many people think as I do. One article I found by jazz writer Harvey Pekar (who unfortunately passed away at age 70 in 2010) wrote precisely what I think about Wynton. The similarities between our viewpoints are uncanny. His article, "The Downside of Wynton Marsalis: The trumpeter is not the jazz savior he's made out to be," can be found at Isthmus dotcom. For even further reading, I also recommend "Trumpeting Mediocrity: Was Wynton Marsalis ever that good?" By Fred Kaplan over at Slate.

THE ARTICLE

A prelude to the artists; Trumpeter Miles Davis really needs no introduction; he is the most recognized name in jazz music worldwide and is the best selling jazz musician of all-time. His professional career spans more than forty-plus years in music. Classical and jazz trumpeter Wynton Marsalis is the self-proclaimed new voice of jazz music and, at the same time, a jazz conservative who wants to preserve the original sound of the music. He is the "Artistic Director of Jazz" at the Lincoln Center in New York City.

Can you imagine if Cuban son montuno never evolved into mambo that later spawned salsa? Can you imagine if the blues never evolved into jazz or if the fusion of the two never evolved into rhythm and blues, which later spawned soul? Imagine if disco never turned into house music, which spawned techno; rock into punk, metal, grunge, and alternative. The point is, by nature, music is supposed to evolve.

Miles Davis changed jazz music at least four times, possibly six. I understand that Miles did what he did to keep the music fresh and relevant in current times. It's understandable why he didn't want to keep making the "old music" or the old style of jazz. The fact is that music is old. Its audience is aging and continually getting smaller and smaller. It's all in the past, and those times are over now by decades. So it baffles me to see musicians like Wynton Marsalis still living in the past. The great debate of whose side to take between Davis and his viewpoint on evolving the music and Marsalis' view of keeping it with a pre-sixties sound has created probably the biggest divide in the jazz community about what can be categorized as "real jazz." The great debate started when Wynton released an article in *The New York Times* on July 31, 1988, titled "What Jazz Is – and Isn't."

"All these purists are walking around talking about how electrical instruments will ruin music. Bad music is what will ruin music, not the instruments musicians choose to play. I don't see nothing wrong

with electrical instruments as long as you get great musicians who will play them right."

I cannot believe throughout Wynton Marsalis' career how intent he has been on keeping jazz old, and by that, I mean pre-sixties sounding. He seems fixated on putting jazz in the museum even though the music isn't dead yet. It's very pontifical thinking and contradictory him "playing" (no pun intended) like some kind of jazz preserver or curator. He is one of the people responsible for killing the music by trying to hold it back from its inevitable change, from its evolution. It's not for him, a single pompous man with no serious involvement in jazz, to decide what's "real jazz" or suitable jazz, and what's not.

It's not his place to appoint himself as some type of jazz ambassador or educator on something he knows nothing about and then tries to speak on behalf of the majority. Wynton never grew up in the 1910s, '20s, '30s, '40s, or '50s, and he was just a young child in the '60s. The jazz of old is not his music. He couldn't and didn't contribute anything to the genre at those times (I don't think he contributes anything now) because, for one, he wasn't alive during the golden era of the music, during its heyday. Secondly, he is still playing all the old music types and hasn't ever contributed anything new. By definition, if he is not a supporter of or playing any contemporary music, the antonym of that would mean that he is old-fashioned and out-of-date.

"I'm not saying that music isn't good, but it's been done over and over and over again. Wynton's playing their dead shit, the kind of stuff anybody can do."

And don't get me wrong about the old music. I love it, and I love to listen to it. I like to listen to the old cats like Miles, Bird, Dizzy, Trane, Satchmo, Herbie, the Duke, Nat King Cole, etc., but that's just it exactly. I like to listen to them play it because, at the time that they made their albums and tunes, the material was new and innovative. I don't want to listen to second-rate musicians now like Wynton making pre-sixties-esque music or rehash pre-sixties tunes composed by first-rate musicians. If I want to hear the old music, I go to the record store and buy the old albums. There are hundreds, if not a couple of thousand good old albums that I've never heard before that I can delve into any time. If I want the music to take my mind back to that era, I go with the guys who made it at those times and not the guys pretending to know what it was like back then. They can act like they can take me there, but I don't believe they will ever be able to arrest my mind as the real artists could, nor will I give them the chance to try.

I like the new music a lot too. I love to listen to Marcus Miller, Stanley Clarke, Incognito, David Sanborn, and Kenny G. I enjoy my copy of Herbie Hancock's *Future 2 Future*. There's nothing wrong with the new wave of musicians we have around the world now, or the new stuff the older ones are doing. We have critics though protesting and fighting it, proclaiming electric instruments to be taboo for jazz music. Why? People (critics especially) shouldn't get so caught up in the "instrument" used to make the music or the new directions they take the music with those instruments. People should care about whether or not the musician can play that tool to a good enough degree to satisfy their ears.

When Miles was alive, he was just the opposite of Wynton. He was trying to keep the music and himself out of the museum. I don't understand why critics and other musicians were trying so hard to kill off Miles before his time. I believe Wynton was attacking him in the media and press out of jealously. He can never hold a light next to all the significant accomplishments Miles has genuinely done for the genre and his sound. I say Miles has genuine accomplishments because although Wynton may have won many major awards, they are all empty in meaning, aren't they? Miles made jazz standards until he died, and people are still performing his music today, including even some of his newest material.

If Miles were to do an already established jazz standard (such as "'Round Midnight") at any point in time, you could be sure that he would play it to such a degree that it would make the tune an even more popular standard. Wynton, on the other hand, how many jazz standards has he made in his entire career? I don't know of any. Wynton is the kind of person that will listen to and play all the old jazz standards to a lesser degree than those already done before him. Still, he isn't the type that can truly create anything new or innovative that people in the future, let's say about over thirty years from now, will want to play. I feel as though when he passes on, his music will most certainly join him. Miles' contributions have always been on a grand scale. He has always been a forward-thinking and progressive person who would never give up on the pursuit of making good innovative music. He did experiments with the fusing of genres, unafraid before others started following suit. And at times, even when the music got to sound outlandish and out there for some people (upon first hearings during those times, mind you) when you really sit down and dissect that music, it is still jazz at heart, at its core.

"But the more famous he became, the more he started saying things –nasty, disrespectful things– about me, things I've never said about musicians who influenced me and who I had great respect for."

-Miles Davis on Wynton Marsalis
Miles: The Autobiography page 359-360

The real slap in the face came when Wynton shot down Miles in the press but then decides in 1986 Miles is good enough to get on stage with at the Vancouver International Jazz Festival. Miles had attended Juilliard in his youth, and Wynton had gone too. Miles made a soundtrack contribution for a Jack Johnson documentary in 1971, so Wynton decided he had to do it in 2004. What is he trying to prove? He is living in Miles' and others' shadow, and at the same time, he seems intent on trying to prove he is somehow better than his elders of jazz. Everything seems to be a competition with him. As with the Miles situation, he's always trying to get one up on Miles. All of this shows Wynton to be a very two-faced, hypocritical person, even jealous.

Interviewer: *"Is it more difficult to be a musician today than it use to? I know it's different, but is it more difficult?"*

Miles: *"I find giant jazz musicians to be dull, very dull, and lazy. They uh talk about, matter fact the word jazz, it mess me around when I hear it. You know it makes me feel, I feel afraid, you know. That feeling you use to get at September when you go back to school, I get that. You know, cause I wanted to be with other great musicians like Dizzy and Charlie Parker. You know when I was coming up, and I didn't want to be left out of anything, you know, so I came to New York to follow it. And I, you know, I learn, and learn, and learn. It's the same thing now; you don't wanna be left out. You know, you don't wanna have your buddies say, "well, we can't take you Miles cause you ain't playin' nothin'." You know, but you have to make a effort to learn, you can't, you can't play clichés and say other people sold out like uh different musicians I've heard. Like the... Wynton Marsalis I told him you can't say that. You know, it's easy to play what you hear on the records, but if you have any feeling at all, you should wanna, you know... It makes me feel good if I compose something and all the fellas like it, you know."*

-Miles Davis
European interview 1984

Starting out, Wynton wanted to blow up and be a big name jazz musician overnight, you could tell, and at the times when things don't turn out to be a certain way for him, he gets mad, just like a selfish child who always wants something but doesn't deserve it. I think he is self-aware; he is living in the shadow of many people, especially Miles Davis, and he doesn't want to be

85

seen like that. But the more Wynton tries to break loose and makes personal attacks with his words in the media, the more it discredits him as a real musician and a likable person. One thing's for sure; he knows how to play a good game of controversy. I don't think Wynton could get real credible recognition with his jazz music, so Wynton uses controversy and is no stranger to it. On Wynton's Wikipedia bio page, he has more written about him in the "Criticism and controversy" section than in the "Musical accomplishments" section. [Note: Be aware that on 12 May 2015, a Wikipedia contributor, DanJazzy, had deleted 241 words along with their cited references from this section. You can still find the older revision of the page on Wikipedia in the Wynton Marsalis: Revision History.] That should be indication enough that something is wrong with his character. But if Wynton will be discussed by the media, press, and public, and will be on people's minds and coming out their mouths, people are going to be curious to want to listen to his sound just because he is talked about, regardless of if it's good or bad. Any press is good press. It all seems very gimmicky to me.

Wynton's own accomplishments are cheaply earned and empty in meaning. He wins a lot of classical music and jazz awards by catering to and playing to what the white critics want to hear, the kind of people who probably listen to jazz, but they like classical music just as much, if not more. They probably say "Well, Wynton is promoting our music (white classical) quite well, let's give something back to him by voting him best trumpet (over Miles and Dizzy), let's give him this award too." Critics recognized his music mostly and brought it up to its current status, definitely not the people. In the case of people vs. critics, Miles thought that people worldwide are the barometer of what you're doing as a musician, not the critics. We, the people, all know that the big awards are issued by critics on committees but never issued by the people, which is truly a shame.

I don't do many articles about jazz, and should I choose to do more in the future, there's a high probability that I will never down another jazz musician quite like this again. I did it this time

86

to write this piece because I was angered enough by Wynton getting away with murder that I felt compelled to do. There is more I wanted to say, but I think I said enough to make my point. There has to be a stopping point somewhere for me. I want to leave everyone with this final thought. Imagine if jazz never turned avant-garde, free, electric, smooth, acid... We'd be leaving behind lots of great music and musicians just because some dude name Wynton doesn't want it to be heard or thinks it deserves the time of day.

AFTERWARD: THE REBUTTAL

There was a harsh critic of my book about five years ago, and he mainly was so because we have diverging and opposite views. Instead of giving my book a proper critique that one would hope for, he said some disrespectful things with the intent to insult, I believe. The apparent attempt to slight my intelligence and paint a picture of me as being inept as a writer was not admirable. I'm using this afterward to write a public rebuttal because although I have nothing to prove to the so-called online critic David Binder, I'd like to give him and people who think like him a professional reply. I will address his biggest gripes, although not all.

The work that I had spent two years of my life completing was under attack. While I want to share this work, my book with the world by promoting it and getting it into as many interested parties' hands as possible, Binder's unmerited review is counterproductive to my efforts. And I have too much dignity in myself and my work to let this go unchecked. It all stemmed from the then four-page article I wrote on Miles Davis and Wynton Marsalis. I wrote it from an unapologetically black standpoint. The article had gotten under his skin so much to the point that instead of just writing about his grievances with it, which I felt he could not objectively do, he went ahead and destroyed my entire book based on it. I'm wondering if I had omitted those four pages for inclusion, and my book was solely a discography like initially intended, what review score would he have given then? What would he have said? I imagine he would have liked the book more if only that part of it was more palatable. Note: I increased the font size in this revised edition, so the article now spans a few more than four pages.

David Binder's whole write-up and rant fell apart because he showed that he could not relate to me, a black man giving his perspective about black musicians and black music, fubu. Not only that, but he clearly did not understand or could wrap his head around what kind of book this was. He misinterpreted a whole 68-page discography and summary book as being a 68-page article. That's exactly how he judged the book. He said, "This book is filled with opinion; it is, however, exceptionally light on fact, and is a waste of money and time." That is an absolute exaggeration. The article is not even a core part of the book. It only makes up six percent of the book and is the only opinionated writing featured within it. It's just supplemental material I tacked on to make the book meatier by providing some actual reading material, aside from having only discography lists. Six percent, and he dare to claim the book was filled with opinions, the audacity. He makes the article sound like a majority of the book. He tried to hurt my credibility by telling a blatant lie.

So he said his piece about the article. OK, that's on him for not trying to utilize the entire book and use it the way intended. Did he not indulge in looking at some video interviews or listening to audio interviews? Did he not use it to help him find some obscure CDs or collectors' CDs? Did he utilize the appraisal guide? He also said my book was "filled with errors of fact," I highly disagree. My book is a reference guide first and foremost, and that is the bulk of the book and the purpose of why you should be buying it. There's not much in the way of a song or album listing being taken as fiction. That says more about Mr. Binder's comprehension than my writing.

"His article on Wynton vs Miles is equally misinformed and written with unequivocal bias." Oh, you mean like Wynton's viewpoints on what jazz is? On the contrary, I'm not misinformed about anything. I think he (Wynton) is the one that is misinformed because the whole Internet has spelled out how they feel about this man on a grand scale, and he somehow missed all of it. The bias that Mr. Binder refers to is a deep emotion felt by many who think and feel the same way as I do, and with good reason. Mr. Binder also said, "and it's your responsibility, as a writer, to be informed and not just regurgitate a popular opinion that has gone long past its 'best buy' date." It's my thoughts that just so happen to be a popular opinion. I'm not jumping on the bandwagon of dislike. I gave reason after reason why I don't like the guy. And for the record, it's not past its best "by" date because Wynton, for the public record, has never taken back anything he said about jazz or the musicians he castigated. Second, if he did apologize about his past insults to his seniors and peers, he would be turning his back on his 30 years' convictions, and I would forgive him for it.

I didn't write the article for the sake of or to garner attention through controversy. I wrote it because it's what I genuinely believe, and I discovered it just so happens it is reflective and epitomizes what many other journalists on the subject matter think. It's not only me; it's also other jazz musicians, jazz writers, journalists, bloggers, and forums. At the end of my article, I left some additional reading that supported my viewpoints. One of the articles was a lot harsher than mine. You'd think I was talking sweet about the guy compared to that. All these negative criticisms Wynton Marsalis garnered for himself, he brought that on himself. He's his own worst enemy.

For Mr. Binder and anyone else thinking of trying to single me out for what I believe, make sure you come at all these other writers with the same energy as you did me. Check the comments on some articles too, you'll find plenty of commentators have a lot of harsh things to say about the guy. Mr. Binder wants you to believe I am the first who started all negative opinions on Wynton. Here are some additional articles that either straight call Wynton out on his shit or acknowledge that he is the great divide I spoke of in jazz with his controversial neoconservative thinking. These are pre and post my article.

2.9.1997: The Jazz Martyr By Andrew Solomon (The New York Times, Section 6, Page 32)

4.24.1998: The downside of Wynton Marsalis: The trumpeter is not the jazz savior he's made out to be By Harvey Pekar (Isthmus)(Also read the comments section)

1.15.2001: Burns' Jazz Doesn't Swing By William Berlind (Observer)

4.7.2004: Trumpeting Mediocrity: Was Wynton Marsalis ever that good? By Fred Kaplan (Slate)

9.28.2010 Ken Burns Jazz: The War of Episode 10 By George Colligan

8.1.2011: Locking Horns: When Miles Davis Met Wynton Marsalis By Brian Boyles (OffBeat Magazine)

4.28. 2011: 50 great moments in jazz: Wynton Marsalis goes back to basics By John Fordham (The Guardian)(Also read the comments section)

8.2013: My Strong Dislike for Wynton Marsalis and Stanley Crouch (rateyourmusic.com board message)

2.4.2014: Jazz and Its Discontents: A Jazz Musicians' Reflections on the Cult of Wynton Marsalis By Kevin Sun (The Crimson)

11.6.2015: Wynton Marsalis: trumpeting controversial ideas of classicism By Philip Clark (The Guardian)(Also read the comments section)

I had to write this rebuttal because I can't allow someone to try to assassinate my character. I can't listen to these jokers try to pass off my hard work, my book as if it were something else entirely, and misinform the public at large about what it is. That I cannot do. He had spent the better half of his lengthy review going off on a tangent talking about that article. He said, "C'mon Vince Wilburn and the rest of the Miles Davis estate: Publish Miles, The Autobiography (in eBook format) so folks can read the real deal rather than aimless, misinformed and poorly written meanderings like this." Sir, this is a companion guide to the autobiography, not a substitute, and this is not a traditional book you pick up and read from left to right. You are supposed to use it to help you find the music in the autobiography. I think you must have bypassed the introduction when I said as much.

Mr. Binder said to me, "You may call yourself a writer, but beyond a small number of articles for a couple of websites, what experience do you have? What's the depth of your background knowledge?" I wrote enough articles for magazine publications and online. It hasn't only been those websites that I contributed something to. I have two published books out now, with a third on the way. I write about what I know. What's the depth of my knowledge when it comes to Miles? Oh, I don't know. I spent the better part of two years making this book from 2009 to 2011. I reread his autobiography about four times to summarize those 448 pages into eleven (now eighteen) pages and correctly annotate and list those 388 jazz tunes and albums. I spent a long time adequately appraising Miles Davis albums and recordings on a world market so readers could buy with confidence, knowing they are not getting ripped off. I own a little over 40 of his albums, over five of his concert DVDs, and five books about him. I watched every single video interview and listened to all audio interviews with the guy from Japan to Europe to the US. And I even visited the man's grave in The Bronx. If I'm not qualified to make a book on him? Who else? To say I'm not an expert on Miles, that's David's sentiment and belief of me.

Closing out my thoughts on Wynton. He does have the chops and technical skill to play, I must admit to that, but even given that he still isn't playing anything. I think performing music by artists he once castigated or didn't criticize is one of his biggest problems. All those standards he continuously plays, and he still doesn't have any of his own. The tunes he plays has already been done before. He hasn't contributed much, if anything, in my opinion, to the genre. He hasn't innovated anything. If anyone needs chastising, it should be him for his laziness for not having the drive to create or innovate. It's easy to be destructive and tear down other musicians. It isn't easy to create. It's almost synonymous with David Binder attempting to tear down my book.

91

DJ MARC ANTOMATTEI'S TOP 10 MILES DAVIS TUNES

Now this list was tough to make. As of now, these are my favorite Miles Davis tunes of all-time. But as with me before, this list can alternate and shift from time-to-time. My top three tunes come close to one another with choosing what to call my number one. I chose "'Round Midnight" because it was the first Davis tune that I fell in love with (probably also the first time I heard Miles). "Blue In Green" puts me at peace. It could arguably be my favorite tune, depending on my mood. "New Rhumba" has that kick to it that gets me going. Everything else on the list is never short of amazing either. Stream or download these ten tunes and put them into a playlist to make what I deem to be the real "best of Miles Davis."

1) 'Round Midnight (Michel Legrand 1958 arrangement)
   (Album: Pure Jazz)[Label: Verve]
2) Blue In Green
   (Album: Kind of Blue)[Label: Columbia]
3) New Rhumba
   (Album: Miles Ahead)[Label: Columbia]
4) Concierto de Aranjuez, Pts. 1 & 2
   (Album: Sketches of Spain)[Label: Columbia]
5) Tomaas
   (Album: Tutu)[Label: Warner Bros.]
6) Blues For Pablo
   (Album: Miles Ahead)[Label: Columbia]
7) I Loves You Porgy
   (Album: Porgy and Bess)[Label: Columbia]
8) Lament
   (Album: Miles Ahead)[Label: Columbia]
9) It's About That Time
   (In A Silent Way)[Label: Columbia]
10) My Funny Valentine
    (My Funny Valentine)[Label: Columbia]

DJ MARC ANTOMATTEI'S TOP 10 MILES DAVIS ALBUMS

Like my top 10 tunes, these albums may occasionally flip-flop with one another. For the past ten years, I went against the grain and had *Miles Ahead* in front of the modal jazz masterpiece *Kind of Blue* as my number 1. I liked more tunes on *Miles Ahead* and gave them more play. I always thought Miles worked best when he performed under the direction of friend and collaborator Gil Evans. I still do. But on second thought, how can I deny the flawlessly executed, played to perfection *Kind of Blue*? A day before sending this revision to the printers, I switched back to *Kind of Blue*.

1) Kind of Blue [Label: Columbia]
2) Miles Ahead [Label: Columbia]
3) Sketches of Spain [Label: Columbia]
4) Seven Steps: The Complete Columbia Recordings of Miles Davis 1963-1964
5) Porgy and Bess [Label: Columbia]
6) Tutu [Label: Warner Bros.]
7) Sorcerer [Label: Columbia]
8) Cookin' [Label: Prestige]
9) E.S.P. [Label: Columbia]
10) In A Silent Way [Label: Columbia]

DJ MARC ANTOMATTEI'S TOP 10 MILES DAVIS ALBUM COVERS

1) Kind of Blue [Label: Columbia]
2) Sketches of Spain [Label: Columbia]
3) Decoy [Label: Columbia]
4) Porgy and Bess [Label: Columbia]
5) In A Silent Way [Label: Columbia]
6) My Funny Valentine [Label: Columbia]
7) Tutu [Label: Warner Bros.]
8) Miles Davis At Newport 1958 [Label: Columbia]
9) Miles In Berlin [Label: Columbia]
10) Bitches Brew [Label: Columbia]

BIBLIOGRAPHY

Airto Moreira. Wikipedia. http://en.wikipedia.org/wiki/Airto_Moreira (23 Dec 2010)

Alkyer, Frank. 2007. *The Miles Davis Reader.* Hal Leonard Books.

All About Ultimate High Quality CD. CDJapan. https://www.cdjapan.co.jp/feature/uhqcd_allabout (25 Sep 2020)

Amandla (album). Wikipedia. http://en.wikipedia.org/wiki/Amandla_(album) (23 Dec 2010)

Aura (Miles Davis album). Wikipedia. http://en.wikipedia.org/wiki/Aura_(Miles_Davis_album) (23 Dec 2010)

Betty Mabry. Wikipedia. http://en.wikipedia.org/wiki/Betty_Davis (23 Dec 2010)

Bill Evans. Wikipedia. http://en.wikipedia.org/wiki/Bill_Evans (10 Feb 2011)

Billie Holiday. Wikipedia. http://en.wikipedia.org/wiki/Billie_Holiday (23 Dec 2010)

Birth of the Cool. Wikipedia. http://en.wikipedia.org/wiki/Birth_of_the_Cool (10 Feb 2011)

Miles Davis | Birth Of The Cool. All About Jazz. http://www.allaboutjazz.com/php/article.php?id=2237 (23 Dec 2010)

Bitches Brew. Wikipedia. http://en.wikipedia.org/wiki/Bitches_Brew (10 Feb 2011)

Blue Note Records. Wikipedia. http://en.wikipedia.org/wiki/Blue_Note_Records (23 Dec 2010)

Blu-spec CD. Wikipedia. http://www.en.wikipedia.org/wiki/Blu-spec_CD (7 Nov 2010)

Blu-Spec CD: yet another attempt at a high-quality audio format. PS3SACD.com news page. http://www.ps3sacd.com/news.html#_20081105 (7 Nov 2010)

Cannonball Adderley: 'Somethin' Else' : NPR. NPR Music. http://www.npr.org/2011/02/07/4559170/cannonball_adderley_somethin_else (10 Feb 2011)

CD Universe. CD Universe. http://cduniverse.com (1 Mar 2011)

Chano Pozo. Wikipedia. http://en.wikipedia.org/wiki/Chano_Pozo (23 Dec 2010)

Charlie Parker. Wikipedia. http://en.wikipedia.org/wiki/Charlie_parker (23 Dec 2010)

Cicely Tyson. Wikipedia. http://en.wikipedia.org/wiki/Cicely_tyson (10 Feb 2011)

Clark Terry. Wikipedia. http://en.wikipedia.org/wiki/Clark_Terry (23 Dec 2010)

Clifford Brown. Wikipedia. http://en.wikipedia.org/wiki/Clifford_Brown (23 Dec 2010)

Davis, Miles D. 1989. *Miles: The Autobiography.* Simon & Schuster Paperbacks.

Decoy (album). Wikipedia. http://en.wikipedia.org/wiki/Decoy_(album) (23 Dec 2010)

Direct Stream Digital. Wikipedia. http://www.en.wikipedia.org/wiki/Direct_Stream_Digital (7 Nov 2010)

Discogs. Discogs. http://www.discogs.com (1 Mar 2011)

Donna Lee. Wikipedia. http://en.wikipedia.org/wiki/Donna_Lee (10 Feb 2011)

DVD-Audio. Wikipedia. http://en.wikipedia.org/wiki/DVD-Audio (1 Mar 2011)

Elwood Buchanan. Wikipedia. http://en.wikipedia.org/wiki/Elwood_Buchanan (23 Dec 2010)

Fats Navarro. Wikipedia. http://en.wikipedia.org/wiki/Fats_Navarro (23 Dec 2010)

Filles de Kilimanjaro. Wikipedia. http://en.wikipedia.org/wiki/Filles_de_Kilimanjaro (23 Dec 2010)

Foley (musician). Wikipedia. http://en.wikipedia.org/wiki/Foley_(musician) (23 Dec 2010)

Freddie Webster. Wikipedia. http://en.wikipedia.org/wiki/Freddie_Webster (23 Dec 2010)

Gil Evans. Wikipedia. http://en.wikipedia.org/wiki/Gil_Evans (23 Dec 2010)

Gramophone record. Wikipedia. http://en.wikipedia.org/wiki/Gramophone_record (10 Feb 2011)

Hampton Hawes. Wikipedia. http://en.wikipedia.org/wiki/Hampton_Hawes (23 Dec 2010)

HMV Japan. HMV ONLINE. http://www.hmv.co.jp/en/ (1 Mar 2011)

HQCD (Hi Quality CD). HQCD (English). http://www.hqcd.jp/eng.html (7 Nov 2010)

HQCD (High Quality CD). HQCD (Japanese). http://www.hqcd.jp/ (7 Nov 2010)

In a Silent Way. Wikipedia. http://en.wikipedia.org/wiki/In_a_Silent_Way (10 Feb 2011)

Jimi Hendrix. Wikipedia. http://en.wikipedia.org/wiki/Jimi_Hendrix (1 Mar 2010)

John Coltrane. Wikipedia. http://en.wikipedia.org/wiki/John_coltrane (23 Dec 2010)

The Man with the Horn. Wikipedia. http://en.wikipedia.org/wiki/The_Man_with_the_Horn (23 Dec 2010)

Martin Luther King, Jr. Wikipedia. http://en.wikipedia.org/wiki/Martin_Luther_King,_Jr. (23 Dec 2010)

Miami Vice (1984) – Episode List. IMDB. http://www.imdb.com/title/tt0086759/episodes#season-2 (23 Dec 2010)

Miles Davis. Wikipedia. http://en.wikipedia.org/wiki/Miles_davis (23 Dec 2010)

Miles Davis for Honda Scooters. YouTube. http://www.youtube.com/watch?v=s5gYCa2WHiw (23 Dec 2010)

Miles Davis – Tokyo 1964. Roio Blog Archive. http://bigozine2.com/roio/?p=490 (23 Dec 2010)

Miles Henry Davis. Wikipedia. http://en.wikipedia.org/wiki/Miles_Henry_Davis (23 Dec 2010)

Miles in the Sky. Wikipedia. http://en.wikipedia.org/wiki/Miles_in_the_Sky (23 Dec 2010)

MQA. MQA. https://www.mqa.co.uk/ (25 Sep 2020)

Music from Siesta. Wikipedia. http://en.wikipedia.org/wiki/Music_from_Siesta (23 Dec 2010)

On the Corner. Wikipedia. http://en.wikipedia.org/wiki/On_the_Corner (10 Feb 2011)

Paul Chambers. Wikipedia. http://en.wikipedia.org/wiki/Paul_Chambers (23 Dec 2010)

Prestige Records. Wikipedia. http://en.wikipedia.org/wiki/Prestige_Records (23 Dec 2010)

The Return Of A Native Son Bill Boggs Is A Philadelphian By Birth, Breeding And Inclination – Philly.com. Philly.com. http://articles.philly.com/1987-08-30/living/26166424_1_bill-boggs-mayfair-father (12 Feb 2011)

'Round About Midnight. Wikipedia. http://en.wikipedia.org/wiki/%27Round_About_Midnight (10 Feb 2011)

SHM-CD Super High Material CD. SHM-CD Super High Material CD. http://shm-cd.co-site.jp/about/about_e.html (7 Nov 2010)

SHM-CD. Wikipedia. http://www.en.wikipedia.org/wiki/SHM-CD (7 Nov 2010)

Sketches of Spain. Wikipedia. http://en.wikipedia.org/wiki/Sketches_of_Spain (23 Dec 2010)

Someday My Prince Will Come (album). Wikipedia. http://en.wikipedia.org/wiki/Someday_My_Prince_Will_Come_(album) (23 Dec 2010)

Sony Music: News & Information (Blu-Spec CD Press Release). Sony Music Group. http://www.sme.co.jp/pressrelease/images/20081105.pdf (7 Nov 2010)

Sorcerer (Miles Davis album). Wikipedia. http://en.wikipedia.org/wiki/Sorcerer_(Miles_Davis_album) (10 Feb 2011)

Star People. Wikipedia. http://en.wikipedia.org/wiki/Star_People (23 Dec 2010)

Street Smart (film). Wikipedia. http://en.wikipedia.org/wiki/Street_Smart_(film) (23 Dec 2010)

Sugar Ray Robinson and Miles Davis: How a Boxing Legend Inspired a Jazz Legend. Suite101. http://www.suite101.com/content/ray-robinson-and-miles-davis-a34316 (23 Dec 2010)

Super Audio CD. Wikipedia. http://www.en.wikipedia.org/wiki/Super_Audio_CD (7 Nov 2010)

A Tribute to Jack Johnson. Wikipedia. http://en.wikipedia.org/wiki/A_Tribute_to_Jack_Johnson (23 Dec 2010)

Tutu (album). Wikipedia. http://en.wikipedia.org/wiki/Tutu_(album) (23 Dec 2010)

We Want Miles. Wikipedia. http://en.wikipedia.org/wiki/We_Want_Miles (23 Dec 2010)

Wynton Kelly. Wikipedia. http://en.wikipedia.org/wiki/Wynton_Kelly (23 Dec 2010)

You're Under Arrest (Miles Davis album). Wikipedia. http://en.wikipedia.org/wiki/You%27re_Under_Arrest_(Miles_Davis_album) (23 Dec 2010)

ACKNOWLEDGEMENTS

First, I would like to thank God for providing me with a body in excellent health that I can use to work and create. Thanks to photographer Gilles Larrain and his assistant/representative Nadira Husain. They licensed me the Miles Davis photo used for the cover of this book. You are gracious in understanding I'm not an extremely wealthy person, just a solitary young man trying to self-publish his first book.

I want to thank my best friend and mentor here in Japan, Mr. David Gregory, for being the biggest motivator to help me get this book completed, printed, and out. You introduced me to other great help and services I wouldn't have known about otherwise, such as the Japan Writers Conference. To my son Michelangelo Antomattei, you are too young and haven't done anything to help contribute to me completing this book, but I just wanted to say to you that you are always in my thoughts, and have that in print. I thank my father for his everlasting support. To all the Miles Davis fans, enthusiasts, and aficionados around the world. And to those who bought my book, I hope you appreciate and enjoy it!

The Miles Davis Section, Tower Records Shibuya 5F

Tower Records, Shibuya, Tokyo, Japan
The World's Largest Record Store

I conducted a lot of field research at Tower. I had the opportunity to see what's out there physically and in existence for the Miles Davis library. I spent a lot of time sitting on the floor Indian style with my laptop out, pulling CDs off the shelf one-by-one cataloging them. The staff saw me for sure because I was in the way a few times, but they didn't say anything. Thanks go to the Tower Records Shibuya staff, whether they know they are generous or not. They gave me my space to do my thing. Respect.

Additionally, I spent a lot of time in my favorite used record store, Disk Union in Ochanomizu, Tokyo. They have about four or five stores around that particular train station. If you can ever make it to Tokyo, make sure you visit the main store directly in front of Ochanomizu station and their dedicated jazz-only store a few blocks away. Not only were they imperative to my research too, but also my personal life. When I would come across something that I had never seen before or something rare, I would buy it, not only for the sake of completing my book, but also because I wanted it for myself to either listen to or have as a collector's item.

ABOUT THE AUTHOR

Marc Antomattei |'an tō mat tā|, also known as DJ Marc Antomattei, was born in El Paso, Texas, on January 4, 1983. Marc is the youngest of four brothers. His Puerto Rican father, Augustin Antomattei from New York City, was a serviceman in the US Army. His African-American mother, Dorothy Antomattei (née Sims) from Waco, Texas, was a homemaker.

Upon reaching adulthood, Marc enlisted in US Air Force, where on July 31, 2003, he arrived in the Greater Tokyo Area as a serviceman. After being honorably discharged in February 2006, Antomattei remained in Japan. He currently works as a professional DJ, freelance graphic designer, writer, and teacher.

F A C E B O O K: www.facebook.com/djantomattei
Y O U T U B E: www.youtube.com/djantomattei

Questions/Comments?
djantomattei@gmail.com

Miles Dewey Davis III (May 26, 1926 – September 28, 1991)

A special thanks to Miles Davis, may he rest in peace.
For without his accomplishments, my book is meaningless.

www.ingramcontent.com/pod-product-compliance
Lightning Source LLC
Chambersburg PA
CBHW021825090426
42811CB00032B/2025/J